FLAMING LIONESS

Ancient Hymns for Egyptian Goddesses

BY CHELSEA LUELLON BOLTON

Contents

Hymns of Aset

Hymns of Bast

Hymns of Bast-Mut

Hymns of Hethert

Hymns of Menhyt

Hymns of Mut

Hymns of Nebet Het

Hymns of Nit

Hymns of Nut

Hymns of Sekhmet

Hymns of Serqet

Hymns of Seshat

Hymns of Tefnut

Epilogue

Acknowledgements

Thank you to Tamara. L. Siuda for granting permission to include her material from:

- Siuda, Tamara L., The *Ancient Egyptian Prayerbook*, Stargazer Design, 2009.
- Siuda, Tamara L., *Nebt-Het: Lady of the House*, Stargazer Design, 2010.
- Siuda, Tamara L., *The Ancient Egyptian Daybook*, Stargazer Design, 2016.
- Canopic Chest Hymn to Nephthys from the Saite Period: British Museum: Museum Number: EA8539

Thank you to IFAO/Le Caire for their permission to include the material from:

- Cauville, Sylvie, *Le Temple de Dendara : La Porte d'Isis*, Dendara, Cairo: IFAO, 1999.
- El-Saghir, Mohamed and Dominique Valbelle. "Komir. I. - The Discovery of Komir Temple. Preliminary Report. II. - Deux hymnes aux divinités de Komir : Anoukis et Nephthys." *BIFAO* 83 (1983), p. 164-166.
- Goyon, J.-Cl. *Confirmation du pouvoir royal au Nouvel An: Brooklyn Museum Papyrus 47.218.50*, BdE 52, Cairo: IFAO, 1972.
- Inconnu-Bocquillon, Danielle, *Le mythe de la déesse lointaine à Philae*, BdE 132, Le Caire/Cairo: IFAO, 2001.
- Sauneron, Serge, *Esna V: Les fêtes religieuses d'Esna aux derniers siècles du paganisme*, Cairo: IFAO, 1962; 2004.

Thank you to Betsy M. Bryan for her permission to include her material from

- "Hatshepsut and Cultic Revelries in the New Kingdom." *Creativity and Innovation in the Reign of Hatshepsut*, SAOC 69 (2014): 101.

Thank you to University of Oklahoma Press for granting permission to include the excerpt from

- Lesko, Barbara, *The Great Goddesses of Egypt*. University of Oklahoma Press, 1999.

Thank you to Holger Kockelmann, Erich Winter and the Austrian Academy of Sciences for granting permission to include material from:

- Kockelmann, Holger and Erich Winter, *Philae III: Die Zweite Ostkolonnade des Tempels der Isis in Philae. (CO II und CO II K)*, Verlag der Osterreichischen Akademie der Wissenschaften/ Austrian Academy of Sciences, 2016.

Thank you to the Austrian Academy of Sciences for granting permission to include the material from:
- Junker, Hermann, *Der Grosse Pylon des Tempels der Isis in Phila*, Wien: Kommission bei Rudolf M. Rohrer, 1958.

- Junker, Hermann and Erich Winter, *Das Geburtshaus des Tempels der Isis in Phila*, Wien: Kommissionsverlag H. Bohlaus Nachf., 1965.

Thank you to Barbara A. Richter for granting permission for me to include her material from

- Richter, Barbara A., *The Theology of Hathor of Dendera: Aural and Visual Scribal Techniques in the Per-Wer Sanctuary*, Lockwood Press, 2016.

Thank you to John Wiley & Sons Ltd. for granting permission to include material from:

- Kitchen, Kenneth Anderson, *Ramesside Inscriptions: Merenptah and the Late Nineteenth Dynasty: IV*, Blackwell Publishing, 2003.

Thank you to Ahmed M. Mekawy Ouda for granting permission to include his translations from

- Ouda, Ahmed M. Mekawy. "The Canopic Box of NS-'3-RWD (BM EA 8539)." *The Journal of Egyptian Archaeology* 98, no. 1 (2012): 134-137.

Thank you to Tamara L. Siuda.

Thank you to Edward P. Butler for proofreading and translation assistance.

Thank you to all of the Egyptologists who worked so hard to make the information about the Gods and Goddesses of ancient Egypt available to all.

Thank you to Mom, Jeremy, Ami and Dad.

Thank you to Christie B., Liza M., Olya N., Erin C. and Tina K.

Thank you to my patrons on Patreon! Thank you to Christie B.! Thank you for your support!

Introduction

Presented here are hymns and prayers to many Eye Goddesses: Aset, Nebet Het, Sekhmet, Mut, Nut, Seshat, Serqet, Menhyt, Hethert, Nit, Tefnut and Bast. Presented here is a collection of hymns, prayers and inscriptions from the temples of Philae, Dendera, Esna and Komir. There are also some key pieces from other papyri and stela included in this book.

While I have academic degrees, I am not fluent in any language other than English. I was able to translate most of these hymns from French and German using various translation software and dictionaries. In some of my translations I had to reorder or paraphrase the words so that they would make sense in the English language. Because of this, my translations are not always literal word-for-word translations. In the hymns, places of certain locations are spelled differently in French and German. So the spellings of some place names were changed to make the book more cohesive. Two of these places are: Senmet (Senmut; Biggeh) and Kenset (Keneset; Elephantine).

Other work contained in this book were translated by professional Egyptologists who translated their work directly from the hieroglyphs and they (or their publishers) kindly gave me permission to include their work in this volume. For anyone who would like to do further research, all the material has full citations within footnotes and there is a full bibliography at the back of the book.

This book is useful for scholars, translators and modern devotees of the ancient Egyptian Goddesses. I have placed the ancient Egyptian name of each Goddess in the hymns since the material from this volume was initially written in ancient Egyptian language instead of the more popular Greek or Roman derived material. There is a list of name correspondences in the back of the book.

The Eye of Ra is a title and role of many ancient Egyptian Goddesses. These Eye Goddesses protect Ra and all of Egypt from enemies. The Eye Goddesses are associated with cobras, snakes, lionesses, leopards, panthers and cats. They wield magic, weapons and flame to protect all of Egypt against enemies.

The Eye of Ra is a solar goddess associated with the cycles of the sun, solar eclipses, the star Sopdet (Sirius), the Morning Star, and the full moon. All the Eye goddesses are associated with solar rays, flame and starlight—in both restorative and destructive capacities.

The Eye is a primordial goddess often portrayed as a snake, especially a cobra. In one creation myth, Ra (or Ra-Atum) created Shu and Tefnut as well as the Eye Goddess. In the myth, Shu and Tefnut departed and the Eye Goddess went after them. When she returned with Shu and Tefnut, the Eye Goddess wept tears of rage since Ra had created another Goddess in their absence. So Ra, to appease her rage, placed Her as the *Uraeus* (Rearing Cobra) on his forehead. Her tears created humankind.

Each of these cycles can be associated with the myths of the Eye of Ra. These cycles can be associated with anger and appeasement; harm and healing; mourning and transformation and the constant renewal of creation. Each of these themes can be associated with the cycles of the natural phenomena and the different myths associated with them.

The Eye of Ra can be associated with the *Isheru* lakes that were a part of many temples. The Eye Goddess becomes angry with Her father Ra, transforms into a raging lioness and departs Egypt. She wanders the desert and Nubia. Most of the time, a god such as Djehuty (Thoth), Shu or Ptah must retrieve her. When she returns to Egypt, the Eye Goddess is appeased through rituals on the *Isheru* lake. She transforms from her lioness form into the form of a cat or another form of the pacified Goddess. The lioness here is the raging goddess and the cat here is the domesticated animal which helped protect homes and farms from pests as well as helped destroy the Serpent Enemy of the Gods. In the Later periods, the Eye of Ra could also be in the form of a leopard, whose spots represented the stars in the sky.[1]

Many Goddesses had the epithets and all the attributes of the Eye Goddess; these are Aset, Nebet Het, Sekhmet, Hethert, Mut, Bast, Tefnut and many others. These Goddesses could be honored in pairs such as Sekhmet as the Raging Lioness and Mut as the Appeased Goddess. The Eye Goddess can also be in the form of a single deity or the Goddess who takes the form of the lioness.

These Goddesses have a long history. They were honored in ancient Egypt and some even honor them today. May these hymns and inscriptions shine a light on our understanding of these Goddesses so that their aspects, facets and attributes are illuminated in our minds just as they brighten Egypt with their sunlight.

May these hymns enrich your life.

Best Regards,
Chelsea Bolton

---

[1] Pinch, Geraldine, *Egyptian Mythology: A Guide to the Gods, Goddesses and Traditions of Ancient Egypt,* (New York: Oxford University Press, 2004), 128-130 and 131-134.

HYMNS OF ASET

(Auset; Isis)

HYMN OF ASET

Aset, Venerable,
Divine Mother, Lady of Senmet,
Great of Magic, One who resides in Philae,
Regent of Nubia,
Great of Carnage in the Place of Execution,
Fury against the enemies of Her brother,
One who dismembered the adversaries,
Queen of Upper and Lower Egypt,
Female *Ba* more than the Gods,
August Goddess, Mistress of Battle,
Lioness, Mistress of Massacre,
On Top of the Execution spot in Senmet.[2]

---

[2] Inconnu-Bocquillon, Danielle, *Le mythe de la déesse lointaine à Philae*, BdE 132, (Le Caire/Cairo: IFAO, 2001), 26.

HYMN OF ASET

Long live the Female Heru,
Powerful Sovereign, Regent of Egypt
Great Flame, Descended from Ra,
Wepeset,
Who protects Nubia,
Her heart comes to the Banks of Heru,
She stands on the Hill, High in Senmet
After Her Majesty has moved away from fury,
She sits in Philae on Her behalf,
Of Hethert, Queen of Upper and Lower Egypt
Aset, the Venerable, Divine Mother.[3]

---

[3] Inconnu-Bocquillon, Danielle, *Le mythe de la déesse lointaine à Philae, BdE 132*, (Le Caire/Cairo: IFAO, 2001), 27.

HYMN OF ASET

Aset, Who Gives Life,
Lady of Philae, Regent and Lady of the Abaton,
August and Powerful, Regent of Nubia
Mistress of the Southern Foreign Lands,
Excellent Sovereign at the Head of...
Queen of Upper and Lower Egypt,
Female *Ra*, Regent of the Two Lands
Venerable, the Great,
Whose likeness does not exist,
August and Powerful,
Whom no one resembles
Daughter of Geb, Child of Nut,
Heiress of the Two Lands when She was born,
She is the Sovereign of Egypt, when She is yet in the swaddling
    clothes
Her Father Shu glorifies Her Majesty,
Ra, Himself is jubilant for Her *Ka*,
Gods and Goddesses are in adoration about Her face,
Pat and *Rekhit* are in love for Her *Ba*,
Aset, Who Gives Life, Lady of Philae.[4]

---

[4] Inconnu-Bocquillon, Danielle, *Le mythe de la déesse lointaine à Philae, BdE 132*, (Le Caire/Cairo: IFAO, 2001), 31.

HYMN OF ASET

Aset, Lady of Flame
Queen of Upper and Lower Egypt,
Similar to Heaven and Earth
Great of Love, Regent of the Two Lands
Sekhmet of Yesterday, Bast of Today
Aset, Who Gives Life, Lady of the Abaton.[5]

---

[5] Inconnu-Bocquillon, Danielle, *Le mythe de la déesse lointaine à Philae, BdE 132*, (Le Caire/Cairo: IFAO, 2001), 35.

HYMN OF ASET

Aset, Who Gives Life, Lady of Philae,
Regent and Lady of the Abaton,
August and Powerful, One Who is at the Head of Nubia,
Great of Magic, Regent of all the Gods,
Mistress of the *Per Wer*
Regent of *Per Neser*,
Holy of Seat in the *Per Nu*,
Queen of Upper and Lower Egypt,
Female Ra, Regent of the Two Lands,
Venerable and Powerful,
One Whose equal does not exist,
Venerable Coiled One on the Head of the One of the Horizon
    (Ra),
She who repels Apep with the formulas of glorifications
Which are in Her mouth;
One who gets up every day with Her Father Ra,
Aset, Who Gives Life, Lady of the Abaton.[6]

---

[6] Inconnu-Bocquillon, Danielle, *Le mythe de la déesse lointaine à Philae*, BdE 132, (Le Caire/Cairo: IFAO, 2001), 40.

HYMN OF ASET

Aset, Who Gives Life,
Lady of the Abaton,
Regent and Lady of Philae,
Wepeset, Lady of Flame,
Regent of the Castle of Flame,
Sekhmet, the Flame
One Who annihilates the enemies of Her brother
The opponents and aggressors of the One of the Horizon,
Queen of Upper and Lower Egypt, more *Ba* than the Gods,
Venerable, More Excellent than the Goddesses,
Without pity against the enemies of Her brother,
The adversaries depart at Her order,
Flame, Mighty One, Who keeps Wandering Demons away,
Aset, Who Gives Life, Lady of the Abaton.[7]

---

[7] Inconnu-Bocquillon, Danielle, *Le mythe de la déesse lointaine à Philae*, BdE 132, (Le Caire/Cairo: IFAO, 2001), 40.

Hymn of Aset

Aset, Who Gives Life, Lady of the Abaton,
August, Regent of Philae,
Venerable and Powerful, Regent of the Gods,
The Beautiful Name,
One Who is at the Head of the Goddesses,
Excellent of Advice,
She Who repels Apep with the formulas of glorification
Which are in Her mouth;
Aset will be appeased in Senmet.[8]

---

[8] Inconnu-Bocquillon, Danielle, *Le mythe de la déesse lointaine à Philae, BdE 132*, (Le Caire/Cairo: IFAO, 2001), 41.

HYMN OF ASET

Aset, Who Gives Life, Lady of the Abaton,
Regent and Lady of Philae,
August and Powerful, Mistress of the Southern Foreign Lands,
Sekhmet, the Flame,
One Who annihilates the enemies of Her brother,
The aggressors and adversaries of the One of the Horizon,
Princess, Regent of the Two Lands,
Powerful, at the Head of the Goddesses,
Sovereign in Heaven, Sovereign on Earth,
Female Ra in the Orb of the Sky,
Mistress of the Melee,
The House is relatively stable, She has Her Stick,
She is invoked on the Day of Combat,
Venerable Protectress,
To Whom no one is similar
Who protects the fearful
And all those whom She loves
in the arena,
What comes out from Her mouth comes to be,
All the Gods are at Her command,
Great of Magic,
One Who is stable in the Venerable Palace,
The Lord appears on His throne at Her command,
Aset is in the form of Wepeset in Senmet,
To protect Her brother Wesir,
To save His majesty,
To make His body safe and sound,
To preserve His mummy inside that Whose Shape is Hidden,

To repel those who are hostile against Him,

To repel the conspirators,

To drive out the enemies of His House,

She will be the Lady of Flame in the Castle of Flame,

One who burns the enemies with the burning breath in the High
Hill.[9]

---

[9] Inconnu-Bocquillon, Danielle, *Le mythe de la déesse lointaine à Philae, BdE 132*, (Le Caire/Cairo: IFAO, 2001), 44.

HYMN OF ASET

Aset, Venerable, Divine Mother
Lady of Philae, She Who Gives Life,
Regent of the Abaton,
Great in Heaven, Powerful on Earth,
One bringing the revenue of the whole world,
Venerable protector of Her son Heru,
Who puts Her terror to the extreme limits of the world,
Sekhmet, the Flame,
One Who annihilates the enemies of Her brother,
The aggressors and the adversaries of the One of the Horizon,
As long as the Mistress of the Human Race will appear in front of
    the Palace
And will be powerful in Her seat,
Philae,
To destroy the enemies,
To punish the aggressors,
To repel the revolts of Egypt,
To make sure that the rebels are massacred
To go through the Place of Torture,
To consume their bodies with Her flame,
She is Wepeset, Lady of Flame in the Castle of Flame,
One who sets ablaze the attackers of the Ennead.[10]

---

[10] Inconnu-Bocquillon, Danielle, *Le mythe de la déesse lointaine à Philae, BdE 132*, (Le Caire/Cairo: IFAO, 2001), 46.

HYMN OF ASET

Aset, Venerable, Divine Mother,
Lady of Philae,
With a cold face against the enemies of Her brother,
Painful of Fiery Heat,
Who is equipped with the sharpened knife,
As long as the Eye of Heru is alive,
Rich of fiery heat,
Painful heat will burn the aggressors,
To consume the revolts,
To consume the enemies of Her brother,
She is like the Eye of Ra,
Lady of Flame, Great of Teeth,
One with the Red Eyes.[11]

---

[11] Inconnu-Bocquillon, Danielle, *Le mythe de la déesse lointaine à Philae*, BdE 132, (Le Caire/Cairo: IFAO, 2001), 50.

HYMN OF ASET

Aset, Venerable, Divine Mother
Lady of Philae, One Who Gives Life
Lady of the Abaton,
Mistress of the Southern Foreign Lands.[12]

---

[12] Inconnu-Bocquillon, Danielle, *Le mythe de la déesse lointaine à Philae, BdE 132*, (Le Caire/Cairo: IFAO, 2001), 58.

HYMN OF ASET

Aset, Who Gives Life,
Lady of the Abaton,
Regent and Lady of Philae,
August and Powerful,
Who protects Her brother against the enemies,
As long as the Divine Mother is at the Head of Philae,
Venerable in the Beginning of the Earth,
To receive joy,
To rejoice
To see Her son in His form,
She will be in the form of the venerable Sekhmet,
Powerful against enemies,
Making the protection of Her brother in Senmet.[13]

---

[13] Inconnu-Bocquillon, Danielle, *Le mythe de la déesse lointaine à Philae*, BdE 132, (Le Caire/Cairo: IFAO, 2001), 58.

HYMN OF ASET

Aset, One Who Gives Life,
Lady of the Abaton,
Regent and Lady of Philae,
Eye of Ra, Mistress of the Sky,
Regent of All the Gods,
In fury against the enemies of Her brother.[14]

---

[14] Inconnu-Bocquillon, Danielle, *Le mythe de la déesse lointaine à Philae, BdE 132*, (Le Caire/Cairo: IFAO, 2001), 63.

HYMN OF ASET

Aset, Venerable, Lady of the Abaton,
Great of Carnage among the enemies of Her brother,
Queen of Upper and Lower Egypt,
More *Ba* than the Gods,
August and Sovereign of the Goddesses,
Furious against the enemies of Her son,
Enemies are aflame,
Powerful, Regent of the Emissaries,
Aset, Who Gives Life, Lady of the Abaton.[15]

---

[15] Inconnu-Bocquillon, Danielle, *Le mythe de la déesse lointaine à Philae, BdE 132*, (Le Caire/Cairo: IFAO, 2001), 66.

HYMN OF ASET

Aset, Divine Mother,
Lady of Philae, Mistress of Terror,
One Whom the Gods adore,
Red One, Mistress of the Red Cloth,
Who loves brightness
She who wards off the enemies,
Mistress of Brightness
At the place of rage.[16]

---

[16] Inconnu-Bocquillon, Danielle, *Le mythe de la déesse lointaine à Philae, BdE 132*, (Le Caire/Cairo: IFAO, 2001), 67.

HYMN OF ASET

Venerable, Female Heru,
At the beginning,
Who is More High than the Gods and Goddesses,
Female *Ka*, Superior of the *Kau*,
Daughter of the Universal Lord Ra,
Divine Eye of Heru, the Great
Great of Magic, One Who resides in the august palace,
Whose face is shining as gold,
Uraeus Snake inside the Palace,
Queen of Upper and Lower Egypt,
Aset, Venerable, Divine Mother
Lady of Philae,
She Who Gives Life, Lady of the Abaton,
Regent and Mistress of the Southern Foreign Lands,
Sovereign in the North,
She Gives the Two Lands the Banks and all that exists.[17]

---

[17] Inconnu-Bocquillon, Danielle, *Le mythe de la déesse lointaine à Philae, BdE 132*, (Le Caire/Cairo: IFAO, 2001), 73.

HYMN OF ASET

August and Powerful
Come in Peace,
To appease the heart of Your Father Ra,
Mistress of the Wig, Regent of the Horned Crown
Female Disk is the counterpart of the Male Disk
One with the Beautiful Face and the painted eyes,
Aset, Who Gives Life, Lady of the Abaton,
Regent and Lady of Philae.[18]

---

[18] Inconnu-Bocquillon, Danielle, *Le mythe de la déesse lointaine à Philae, BdE 132*, (Le Caire/Cairo: IFAO, 2001), 79.

HYMN OF ASET

Aset, Who Gives Life,
Lady of the Abaton,
First One, Born in the Beginning,
Sekhmet, the Flame,
One who annihilates the enemies of Her brother,
The aggressors and adversaries of the One of the Horizon,
Princess, Regent of Philae,
Powerful at the Head of the Goddessess,
Daughter of Geb, Whose likeness does not exist,
Female Ra in the Four Regions of the Sky.[19]

---

[19] Inconnu-Bocquillon, Danielle, *Le mythe de la déesse lointaine à Philae*, BdE 132, (Le Caire/Cairo: IFAO, 2001), 84.

HYMN OF ASET

Aset, One Who Gives Life,
Lady of the Abaton,
Regent and Lady of Philae,
Eye of Ra, Mistress of the Sky,
Regent of All the Gods,
Queen of Upper and Lower Egypt,
Female Ra of the Two Lands (*Raet tawy*),
Mighty One,
Whose likeness does not exist,
Unique in Heaven, Without Equal,
Aset, Who Gives Life,
Lady of the Abaton,
August and Perfect,
Regent in the Castle of the Front.[20]

---

[20] Inconnu-Bocquillon, Danielle, *Le mythe de la déesse lointaine à Philae, BdE 132*, (Le Caire/Cairo: IFAO, 2001), 91.

HYMN OF ASET

Aset, One Who Gives Life,
Lady of the Abaton,
Regent and Lady of Philae,
Sovereign in Heaven, Princess on Earth,
One Who protects Her brother in all the nomes.[21]

---

[21] Inconnu-Bocquillon, Danielle, *Le mythe de la déesse lointaine à Philae*, BdE 132, (Le Caire/Cairo: IFAO, 2001), 93.

HYMN OF ASET

Aset, One Who Gives Life,
Lady of the Abaton,
Regent and Lady of Philae,
Protector, Mistress of Protection,
Who protects the One
Who is at the Head of His Bed (Wesir),
One Who watches over Ra, everyday.[22]

---

[22] Inconnu-Bocquillon, Danielle, *Le mythe de la déesse lointaine à Philae, BdE 132*, (Le Caire/Cairo: IFAO, 2001), 94.

HYMN TO ASET

Aset, Giver of Life
Lady of Philae, Excellent Sister of the God
In the midst of the Abaton,
Born in Dendera in the Night of the Child in His Nest,
So that jubilation arises throughout the country.[23]

---

[23] Kockelmann, Holger and Erich Winter, *Philae III: Die Zweite Ostkolonnade des Tempels der Isis in Philae. (CO II und CO II K)*, (Verlag der Osterreichischen Akademie der Wissenschaften/Austrian Academy of Sciences, 2016), 16. Translated by Chelsea Bolton. I changed Isis to her ancient Egyptian name Aset.

HYMN TO ASET

Aset, the Great, Mother of God
Lady of the Two Lands,
Princess of all the Gods,
Princess, Lady of the Fruit Country,
Lady of the Field,
Who makes the flowers emerge:
the green leaves and the papyrus.
Lady of Prosperity.[24]

---

[24] Kockelmann, Holger and Erich Winter, *Philae III: Die Zweite Ostkolonnade des Tempels der Isis in Philae. (CO II und CO II K)*, (Verlag der Osterreichischen Akademie der Wissenschaften/Austrian Academy of Sciences, 2016), 54. Translated by Chelsea Bolton. I changed Isis to her ancient Egyptian name Aset.

HYMN OF ASET

Ba more powerful than that of the Gods
Glorious One, Who raised the Goddesses
Those with a flushed face at the enemies of their son
At whose command corruption comes forth
Powerful Flame Goddess,
Princess of the Wandering Daemons
Aset, the Giver of Life, Lady of the Abaton.[25]

---

[25] Kockelmann, Holger and Erich Winter, *Philae III: Die Zweite Ostkolonnade des Tempels der Isis in Philae. (CO II und CO II K)*, (Verlag der Osterreichischen Akademie der Wissenschaften/Austrian Academy of Sciences, 2016), 57. Translated by Chelsea Bolton. I changed Isis to her ancient Egyptian name Aset.

Hymn of Aset

Ruler of Egypt
Great Sun Goddess on Earth,
Queen is She in the Four Corners of the Sky,
Aset, the Giver of Life, Lady of Philae,
Glorious One, Powerful One,
Princess of the Southern Foreign Lands.[26]

---

[26] Kockelmann, Holger and Erich Winter, *Philae III: Die Zweite Ostkolonnade des Tempels der Isis in Philae. (CO II und CO II K)*, (Verlag der Osterreichischen Akademie der Wissenschaften/Austrian Academy of Sciences, 2016), 60. Translated by Chelsea Bolton. I changed Isis to her ancient Egyptian name Aset.

HYMN OF ASET

Aset, the Giver of Life,
Lady of Philae,
Sister, Who watches over Her brother,
Protector of Her brother in His sanctuary,
Who hides His body in the Abaton.[27]

---

[27] Kockelmann, Holger and Erich Winter, *Philae III: Die Zweite Ostkolonnade des Tempels der Isis in Philae. (CO II und CO II K)*, (Verlag der Osterreichischen Akademie der Wissenschaften/Austrian Academy of Sciences, 2016), 79. Translated by Chelsea Bolton. I changed Isis to her ancient Egyptian name Aset.

HYMN OF ASET

Aset, the Great, Mother of God
Lady of Philae, Lady of Terror
Praise the Gods
Red One, Lady of the Red Cloth,
Who overthrows the enemies
Lady of Pleasure in place of wrath's red.[28]

---

[28] Kockelmann, Holger and Erich Winter, *Philae III: Die Zweite Ostkolonnade des Tempels der Isis in Philae. (CO II und CO II K)*, (Verlag der Osterreichischen Akademie der Wissenschaften/Austrian Academy of Sciences, 2016), 80. Translated by Chelsea Bolton. I changed Isis to her ancient Egyptian name Aset.

HYMN OF ASET

Aset, Giver of Life, Lady of Abaton,
Mother of God, Princess of the Gods and Goddesses,
Great *Djedet* of Her brother Wesir,
The Water Libationer, who pours water for his *ba*.[29]

---

[29] Kockelmann, Holger and Erich Winter, *Philae III: Die Zweite Ostkolonnade des Tempels der Isis in Philae. (CO II und CO II K)*, (Verlag der Osterreichischen Akademie der Wissenschaften/Austrian Academy of Sciences, 2016), 85. Translated by Chelsea Bolton. I changed Isis to her ancient Egyptian name Aset. I changed Osiris to his ancient Egyptian name Wesir.

HYMN OF ASET

Princess in Philae,
Beautiful in Appearance in Philae
Lady of the *Uraeus* Snake, Princess of the Cobra,
On whose command the King appears,
Aset, Giver of Life, Lady of Philae.[30]

---

[30] Kockelmann, Holger and Erich Winter, *Philae III: Die Zweite Ostkolonnade des Tempels der Isis in Philae. (CO II und CO II K)*, (Verlag der Osterreichischen Akademie der Wissenschaften/Austrian Academy of Sciences, 2016), 251-252. Translated by Chelsea Bolton. I changed Isis to her ancient Egyptian name Aset.

HYMN OF ASET

Aset, Giver of Life, Lady of Philae
Daughter of Geb, Born of Nut
Ruler, Princess of the Goddesses,
Ruler,
Aset, Giver of Life, Lady of Philae
Lady of the Southern Foreign Lands.[31]

---

[31] Kockelmann, Holger and Erich Winter, *Philae III: Die Zweite Ostkolonnade des Tempels der Isis in Philae. (CO II und CO II K)*, (Verlag der Osterreichischen Akademie der Wissenschaften/Austrian Academy of Sciences, 2016), 92. Translated by Chelsea Bolton. I changed Isis to her ancient Egyptian name Aset.

HYMN OF ASET

Aset, Giver of Life, Lady of Abaton
Princess, Lady of Philae,
Ruler in the Sky like Ra
Great and Powerful, Princess of the Gods
At whose sight Ra is happy every day.[32]

---

[32] Kockelmann, Holger and Erich Winter, *Philae III: Die Zweite Ostkolonnade des Tempels der Isis in Philae. (CO II und CO II K)*, (Verlag der Osterreichischen Akademie der Wissenschaften/Austrian Academy of Sciences, 2016), 145-146. Translated by Chelsea Bolton. I changed Isis to her ancient Egyptian name Aset.

HYMN OF ASET

Great Falcon Goddess, Powerful One,
Princess of the Gods and Goddesses,
Aset, the Great, Mother of God
Lady of Philae, the Guardian.[33]

---

[33] Kockelmann, Holger and Erich Winter, *Philae III: Die Zweite Ostkolonnade des Tempels der Isis in Philae. (CO II und CO II K)*, (Verlag der Osterreichischen Akademie der Wissenschaften/Austrian Academy of Sciences, 2016), 208. Translated by Chelsea Bolton. I changed Isis to her ancient Egyptian name Aset.

HYMN OF ASET

Aset, the Great, Princess of Philae
Great Goddess,
Lady of Upper and Lower Egypt
Ruler in the Two Lands.[34]

---

[34] Kockelmann, Holger and Erich Winter, *Philae III: Die Zweite Ostkolonnade des Tempels der Isis in Philae. (CO II und CO II K)*, (Verlag der Osterreichischen Akademie der Wissenschaften/Austrian Academy of Sciences, 2016), 274. Translated by Chelsea Bolton. I changed Isis to her ancient Egyptian name Aset.

HYMN OF ASET

Lady of All Egypt, Princess of the Whole Earth
You praise Your *ka* in the districts and cities
Aset, Giver of Life, Lady of Philae.[35]

---

[35] Kockelmann, Holger and Erich Winter, *Philae III: Die Zweite Ostkolonnade des Tempels der Isis in Philae. (CO II und CO II K)*, (Verlag der Osterreichischen Akademie der Wissenschaften/Austrian Academy of Sciences, 2016), 278. Translated by Chelsea Bolton. I changed Isis to her ancient Egyptian name Aset.

HYMN OF ASET

Aset, Lady of Philae,
Eye of Ra, Princess,
Lady of Abaton,
Princess,
Lady of the Southern Foreign Lands.[36]

---

[36] Kockelmann, Holger and Erich Winter, *Philae III: Die Zweite Ostkolonnade des Tempels der Isis in Philae. (CO II und CO II K)*, (Verlag der Osterreichischen Akademie der Wissenschaften/Austrian Academy of Sciences, 2016), 270. Translated by Chelsea Bolton. I changed Isis to her ancient Egyptian name Aset.

HYMN TO ASET

Great Falcon Goddess from the Beginning,
Who has risen above the Gods and Goddesses
The *Ka-force* that dominates the other *Ka-forces*,
Daughter of the Lord of All
Divine Eye of the Great God,
Great of Magic in the middle of the Great Temple.
Uraeus of the brightest gold
Uraeus Snake in the middle of the Temple,
Queen of Upper and Lower Egypt,
Lady of Philae, Giver of Life
Lady of the Abaton,
Princess, Lady of the Southern Foreign Lands
Ruler of the North.[37]

---

[37] Kockelmann, Holger and Erich Winter, *Philae III: Die Zweite Ostkolonnade des Tempels der Isis in Philae. (CO II und CO II K)*, (Verlag der Osterreichischen Akademie der Wissenschaften/Austrian Academy of Sciences, 2016), 235-236. Translated by Chelsea Bolton. I changed Isis to her ancient Egyptian name Aset. It says Great Palace, but it said they meant Great Temple, so I put Temple here.

HYMN OF ASET

Lady of the Temple
Ruler over the Words of God,
Glorious One, Powerful One
Princess of the Southern Foreign Lands,
Aset, the Great, Mother of God
Ruler in the Land of Atum.[38]

---

[38] Kockelmann, Holger and Erich Winter, *Philae III: Die Zweite Ostkolonnade des Tempels der Isis in Philae. (CO II und CO II K)*, (Verlag der Osterreichischen Akademie der Wissenschaften/Austrian Academy of Sciences, 2016), 102. Translated by Chelsea Bolton. I changed Isis to her ancient Egyptian name Aset.

HYMN OF ASET

Aset, Giver of Life
Lady of Philae,
Sun Goddess, Aset as Her Father's Protector,
The One sitting on the Throne of Egypt.[39]

---

[39] Kockelmann, Holger and Erich Winter, *Philae III: Die Zweite Ostkolonnade des Tempels der Isis in Philae. (CO II und CO II K)*, (Verlag der Osterreichischen Akademie der Wissenschaften/Austrian Academy of Sciences, 2016), 277. Translated by Chelsea Bolton. I changed Isis to her ancient Egyptian name Aset.

Hymn of Aset

Aset, Giver of Life, Lady of Abaton
Princess, Lady of Philae
Ruler in Heaven, Ruler on Earth
Her brother in all the districts, glorified.[40]

---

[40] Kockelmann, Holger and Erich Winter, *Philae III: Die Zweite Ostkolonnade des Tempels der Isis in Philae. (CO II und CO II K)*, (Verlag der Österreichischen Akademie der Wissenschaften/Austrian Academy of Sciences, 2016), 244. Translated by Chelsea Bolton. I changed Isis to her ancient Egyptian name Aset.

HYMN OF ASET

Aset, Giver of Life, Lady of Abaton
Princess, Lady of Philae,
Great in Heaven, Powerful on Earth
Ruler in the Circuit of the Sun.[41]

---

[41] Kockelmann, Holger and Erich Winter, *Philae III: Die Zweite Ostkolonnade des Tempels der Isis in Philae. (CO II und CO II K)*, (Verlag der Osterreichischen Akademie der Wissenschaften/Austrian Academy of Sciences, 2016), 285. Translated by Chelsea Bolton. I changed Isis to her ancient Egyptian name Aset.

HYMN OF ASET

Aset, the Great, Mother of God
Lady of Philae,
Magnificent, Powerful One
Princess of the Gods and Goddesses.[42]

---

[42] Kockelmann, Holger and Erich Winter, *Philae III: Die Zweite Ostkolonnade des Tempels der Isis in Philae. (CO II und CO II K)*, (Verlag der Osterreichischen Akademie der Wissenschaften/Austrian Academy of Sciences, 2016), 294-295. Translated by Chelsea Bolton. I changed Isis to her ancient Egyptian name Aset.

HYMN OF ASET

Aset, Who Gives Life to the King,
the Great, Mother of God
With the Sacred Place at the Head of Philae
Ruler in the Temples,
Who makes the Mystery of Her son Heru endure
Who drives away the wandering daemon, akhu and the dead.
She is Satet, the Princess
Lady of the Beginning of the Year
According to whom the King is established,
On Whose tongue is the writing of Djehuty.[43]

---

[43] Kockelmann, Holger and Erich Winter, *Philae III: Die Zweite Ostkolonnade des Tempels der Isis in Philae. (CO II und CO II K)*, (Verlag der Osterreichischen Akademie der Wissenschaften/Austrian Academy of Sciences, 2016), 303-304. Translated by Chelsea Bolton. I changed Isis to her ancient Egyptian name Aset.

HYMN OF ASET

Aset, the Great, Mother of God
Lady of Philae, Giver of Life
Lady of Abaton,
Mourning Woman,
Who cares about the secret figure of Her brother
Princess of the Gods,
With an exalted name among the Goddesses,
Magic Snake,
Without whose knowledge you cannot enter the palace (become
    King)
the Lord (King) appears at Her command.[44]

[44] Kockelmann, Holger and Erich Winter, *Philae III: Die Zweite Ostkolonnade des Tempels der Isis in Philae. (CO II und CO II K)*, (Verlag der Osterreichischen Akademie der Wissenschaften/Austrian Academy of Sciences, 2016), 310-311. Translated by Chelsea Bolton. I changed Isis to her ancient Egyptian name Aset.

HYMN OF ASET

Temet, the Princess of the Two Lands,
She from Whose leg the Nile pours in its time,
Perfect *Djedet*, Who grows the plants
Who makes the land green, with what it has produced;
When She rises, all growth greens
Aset, Giver of Life, Lady of Abaton.[45]

---

[45] Kockelmann, Holger and Erich Winter, *Philae III: Die Zweite Ostkolonnade des Tempels der Isis in Philae. (CO II und CO II K)*, (Verlag der Osterreichischen Akademie der Wissenschaften/Austrian Academy of Sciences, 2016), 255-256. Translated by Chelsea Bolton. I changed Isis to her ancient Egyptian name Aset. Thank you to Tamara L. Siuda for her help with this translation.

HYMN OF ASET

Aset, Giver of Life, Lady of Abaton
Princess, Lady of Philae
Excellent Queen
Princess of the Circuit of the Sun
All foreign lands behave according
To what She commanded.

Glorious One, Powerful One
Uraeus of the Gods and Goddesses
Great in the Sky, Powerful on Earth
Beautiful of appearance in all the nomes.[46]

---

[46] Kockelmann, Holger and Erich Winter, *Philae III: Die Zweite Ostkolonnade des Tempels der Isis in Philae. (CO II und CO II K)*, (Verlag der Osterreichischen Akademie der Wissenschaften/Austrian Academy of Sciences, 2016), 103-104. Translated by Chelsea Bolton. I changed Isis to her ancient Egyptian name Aset.

HYMN OF ASET

Aset, Giver of Life, Lady of Abaton
Princess, Lady of Philae
Seshat, the Great, Princess of the Library
Great of Magic, Princess of All the Gods.[47]

---

[47] Kockelmann, Holger and Erich Winter, *Philae III: Die Zweite Ostkolonnade des Tempels der Isis in Philae. (CO II und CO II K)*, (Verlag der Osterreichischen Akademie der Wissenschaften/Austrian Academy of Sciences, 2016), 143. Translated by Chelsea Bolton. I changed Isis to her ancient Egyptian name Aset.

HYMN OF ASET-SOPDET

Sopdet (Satet), the Great, Lady of Elephantine
Lady of the Bow, with Swift Arrows
With an angry heart and anger-ridden eyes
Who overthrows the enemy of her brother, Wesir.
Magnificent of the Sky,
Powerful One, Princess
Of the Nome of the Two Meret Goddesses
Who dispels the enemies and Set's comrades
Sopdet, the Great.[48]

---

[48] Kockelmann, Holger and Erich Winter, *Philae III: Die Zweite Ostkolonnade des Tempels der Isis in Philae. (CO II und CO II K)*, (Verlag der Osterreichischen Akademie der Wissenschaften/Austrian Academy of Sciences, 2016), 41-42. Translated by Chelsea Bolton. I changed Sirius/Sothis to her ancient Egyptian name Sopdet. I changed Osiris to his ancient Egyptian name Wesir.

ARETALOGY OF ASET

Aset, Mistress of Ta-senet, Lady of the Palace
Who is within the Castle of the *Ba*
I am Aset, Sekhet
Mistress of the Campaign
Beneficent and Perfect in Wp
in My Name of Nebtu
I am the Queen of the Gods in Pi
Mistress of Men
at the head of the House of Life;
I am Seshat, the Great
Head of the House of Books;
Great of Magic,
Lady of the House of the King
I am the Sovereign of Egypt
and I conquer the foreign lands in joy
I am the Mother of the King
Mother of the God Heru
the Royal Wife
the Royal Sister of Wennefer.[49]

---

[49] Sauneron, Serge, *Esna V: Les fêtes religieuses d'Esna aux derniers siècles du paganisme*, (Cairo: IFAO, 1962; 2004), 207-208. Translated by Chelsea Bolton. Thank you to Edward Butler for his help.

BROOKLYN MUSEUM PAPYRUS 47.218.50

Aset the Great, Mother of God
Aset, Great of Magic
Aset, Lady of Humans
Aset Hededyt
Aset-Sopdet, who protects the Two Lands
Aset, with innumerable manifestations
Aset, Lady of Names.[50]

---

[50] Goyon, J.-Cl. *Confirmation du pouvoir royal au Nouvel An: Brooklyn Museum Papyrus 47.218.50, BdE 52*, (Cairo: IFAO, 1972), 65. Translated by Chelsea Bolton.

HYMN FROM CANOPIC BOX OF NS-'3-RWD (BM EA 8539)

Hail to You, Aset, the Great
Mother of the God,
the First Great Royal Wife of her husband
the Wife of the God in the resting place of Mendes
Lady of Stride in the House of Hen
Lady of Offerings in the Cemetery,
Who assembled her husband in Heliopolis
Hesat, Beloved of Her son,
Who placed him on his father's throne,
Who knows things in the portable shrine Chemmis
Lady of Protection in the sacred bark.[51]

---

[51] Ouda, Ahmed M. Mekawy. "The Canopic Box of NS-'3-RWD (BM EA 8539)." *The Journal of Egyptian Archaeology 98, no. 1* (2012): 135. I changed Isis to her ancient Egyptian name Aset.

BIRTHDAY HYMN OF ASET

Aset, this Eldest Daughter of Nut,
Mistress of Magic, the Provider of the Book,
The Mistress Who satisfies the Two Lands,
Her face is glorious,
I am the brother and I am the sister.
The name of this day is 'he who makes terror'.

Aset, the Goddess Who Guides,
The *Akhet* Eye, Daughter of Nut,
Mistress of Chemmis.
Save me from any bad or evil thing.
Save the son Heru on this day.
The name of this day is 'making preparation'.[52]

---

[52] Siuda, Tamara L., The *Ancient Egyptian Daybook*, (Stargazer Design, 2016), 300.

HYMNS OF BAST

(Bastet)

HYMN OF BAST

Lady of the Shrine,
Daughter of Heru,
Residing in the Holy Field (Bubastis).[53]

---

[53] Naville, Edouard Henri, *Bubastis (1887-1889)*, (London: Kegan Paul, Trubner and Co. 57 & 59, 1891), 58.

HYMN OF BAST

Lady of Bubastis,
Daughter of Ra,
Queen of the Sky,
Who Rules over all the Gods,
Great One,
Lady of Bubastis,
Priestess *Heri Sesheta* of Tum,
Only One,
Who has no descent,
the Goddess of the North,
Who rules.[54]

---

[54] Naville, Edouard Henri, *Bubastis (1887-1889)*, (London: Kegan Paul, Trubner and Co. 57 & 59, 1891), 58.

HYMN OF BAST

Bast, Lady of Bubastis,
Eye of Ra,
Mistress of the East,
Who protects Her beloved son, Heru the Child,
Mistress of the Birthplace of Her beloved son.[55]

[55] Junker, Hermann, *Der Grosse Pylon des Tempels der Isis in Phila*, (Wien: Kommission bei Rudolf M. Rohrer, 1958), 256.

HYMN OF BAST

Bast, Lady of Bubastis,
Princess,
Mistress of Philae,
Eye of Ra,
Who gleams on His forehead,
Richly adorned in God's Land.[56]

---

[56] Junker, Hermann and Erich Winter, *Das Geburtshaus des Tempels der Isis in Phila,* (Wien: Kommissionsverlag H. Böhlaus Nachf., 1965), 35.

HYMN OF BAST

Bast, Princess,
Lady of Bubastis,
Worthy One,
Powerful at the Head of the Birth House,
Anat, who protects Her son Heru.[57]

---

[57] Junker, Hermann and Erich Winter, *Das Geburtshaus des Tempels der Isis in Phila*, (Wien: Kommissionsverlag H. Böhlaus Nachf., 1965), 391.

HYMN OF BAST

Bast, Lady of Bubastis
Regent and Lady of Philae,
Eye of Ra,
Who shines on His forehead,
One whose transformations are numerous in the Earth of God.[58]

---

[58] Inconnu-Bocquillon, Danielle, *Le mythe de la déesse lointaine à Philae, BdE 132*, (Le Caire/Cairo: IFAO, 2001), 56.

HYMN OF BAST

Bast, Lady of Bubastis,
Eye of Ra,
Mistress of the Gods,
Great of Magic,
Mother of the God,
Lady of Heaven,
Mistress of Both Lands.[59]

---

[59] Kitchen, Kenneth Anderson, *Ramesside Inscriptions: Merenptah and the Late Nineteenth Dynasty: IV*, (Blackwell Publishing, 2003), 251.

HYMN OF BAST: EXCERPT FROM THE CAIRO CALENDAR

Bast,
who protects the Two Lands,
who cares for him who comes in the darkness.[60]

---

[60] Siuda, Tamara L., *The Ancient Egyptian Daybook*, (Stargazer Design, 2016), 153-154. For the Procession of Bast on 1 Peret 20.

INSCRIPTION FROM BUBASTIS

Bast, Lady of the Shrine and Eye of Heru,
Pre-eminent of the God's Field, Lady of Heaven,
Mistress of All the Gods.[61]

---

[61] Rosenow, Daniela. "The Naos of 'Bastet, Lady of the Shrine' from Bubastis." *The Journal of Egyptian Archaeology* 94, no. 1 (January 2008): 258. I changed Bastet to Bast. I changed Horus to his ancient Egyptian name Heru.

HYMNS OF BAST-MUT

(Mut-Bast)

HYMN OF MUT-BAST OR BAST-MUT

Mut, the Great Bast
Ruler of Karnak,
Mistress of Amiability and Love.[62]

[62] Breasted, James Henry, Ancient *Records of Egypt: The Nineteenth Dynasty Volume III*, (Chicago: University of Chicago Press, 1906), 74. Translated by James Henry Breasted.

HYMN OF BAST-MUT: BROOKLYN MUSEUM PAPYRUS 47.218.50

Bast, Lady of Bubastis
Bast, Eye of Heru
Bast, who resides in the Meadows of the God
Bast, of the Countryside of Bubastis
Bast, of the Place of Her Power
Bast, with innumerable faces
Bast, who presides over the Mysteries
Mut, the Great Lady of *Isheru*.[63]

---

[63] Goyon, J.-Cl. *Confirmation du pouvoir royal au Nouvel An: Brooklyn Museum Papyrus 47.218.50, BdE 52*, (Cairo: IFAO, 1972), 67. Translated by Chelsea Bolton.

HYMNS OF HETHERT

(Hetharu; Hwt Hrw; Hathor)

HYMN OF HETHERT

Hethert, Venerable
Lady of Senmet,
Eye of Ra, Mistress of the Sky,
Regent of All the Gods,
August and Powerful in the Two Lands,
Lady of Flame in the Castle of Flame,
She Who satisfies the Heart of Her Father Ra.[64]

---

[64] Inconnu-Bocquillon, Danielle, *Le mythe de la déesse lointaine à Philae, BdE 132*, (Le Caire/Cairo: IFAO, 2001), 25.

HYMN OF HETHERT

How beautiful is Your face, Temet!
Regent of the Two Lands,
Mistress of the Red Cloth, Who loves brightness,
May You appear in Senmet in order to take possession of the Per
   Wer.
May You take Your place in life, in the House of Rest,
And establish the royalty of Heru, the son of Wesir,
Then You will appear as Hethert,
And Your majesty will settle in Philae,
Aset rejoices in the Place to Deposit Offerings,
Your heart will be intoxicated
When Heru appears on Earth.
Hethert, Venerable,
Lady of Senmet,
Gold of the Gods, Electrum of the Goddesses
August and Powerful,
One who springs from Kenset,
Reaching Senmet in the form of Wepeset,
Venerable,
One who purifies Her members in the Abaton,
And settles there for eternity,
Shu being with Her to create Her perfection,
While Djehuty appeases Her.[65]

---

[65] Inconnu-Bocquillon, Danielle, *Le mythe de la déesse lointaine à Philae, BdE 132*, (Le Caire/Cairo: IFAO, 2001), 55.

HYMN OF HETHERT

Venerable, Female Heru,
Mistress of the Basin of Fire,
August and Great in Heaven and on Earth,
Mistress of Life,
Beautiful Face,
Great of Love in all the Two Lands,
Luminous of the Luminous
Powerful of the Powerful,
Queen of Upper and Lower Egypt
Hethert, Venerable One,
Lady of Senmet, Powerful Sovereign
One Who springs from Kenset,
Who attends Senmet in the form of the Venerable Wepeset,
And rises up.
Flame, Whose burning breath burns the enemies
Angry in Sekhmet, Appeased in Bast,
One who makes the land prosper with Her papyrus of Life,
One who places love beside the Ennead.[66]

---

[66] Inconnu-Bocquillon, Danielle, *Le mythe de la déesse lointaine à Philae*, BdE 132, (Le Caire/Cairo: IFAO, 2001), 72.

HYMN OF HETHERT

How beautiful is Your face,
When You appear in glory!
And You are joyous!
Hethert, Venerable One,
Lady of Senmet,
Hethert, Venerable One,
Lady of the Enclosure of the Call,
Your Father Ra exalts when You awaken,
Your brother, Shu pays homage to Your face,
Djehuty, Powerful in Intoxicating Beer
He calls You, O Powerful One
the Great Ennead is pleased and happy
Baboons are in front of Your face,
They dance for Your majesty,
The Hity play the tambourine for Your Ka,
They sing Your hymns, and worship You,
Henemenet are in awe before Your power,
Men and Women implore You to give them love,
For You, the virgins open the festivities
And give You their protective spirit
You are the Mistress of Praise,
Mistress of Dance, Great in Love,
Mistress of Women and Beauty,
You are the Mistress of Drunkenness, at many festivals,
Mistress of the Frankincense,
Mistress of Braiding the Wreath,
Mistress of the Mirth, Mistress of Exultation,
To the majesty of whom one makes music,

Venerable Female Pillar,

Female *Ba* in Bugem,

You are the Mistress of the Sekhem Sistrum,

Mistress of the Menat and the Seshesh Sistrum,

To Your *Ka*,

From which one raises the Wensheb,

You are the Mistress of Dance,

Mistress of Song and Dance, with the lute,

Whose face shines every day,

One who dispels sorrow,

May You present Your beautiful face.[67]

---

[67] Inconnu-Bocquillon, Danielle, *Le mythe de la déesse lointaine à Philae, BdE 132*, (Le Caire/Cairo: IFAO, 2001), 101. Oliban here can be Frankincense or incense.

HYMN OF HETHERT

Hethert, Venerable One,
Lady of Senmet, Regent and Lady of Philae,
Eye of Ra, Mistress of Heaven,
Regent of All the Gods,
Great of Love,
One Who Rules Over Women,
And who fills the sky and earth with Her perfection,
Mistress of Jubilation,
Regent of Song and Dance
The daily food of Her majesty is drunkenness,
That which comes from Mehyt towards Egypt
Who makes Her seat in Senmet
In the form of Wepeset.
More Luminous than the Luminous Ones,
More Princess than the Princes,
Gold of the Golden Ones,
Regent of the Goddesses,
August and Powerful, issue of Ra,
August Female Ra, Regent of Senmut,
Venerable, Coiled One on the Head of Ra,
She who consumes Her enemies with the burning breath of Her
    mouth.
Mistress of Wine,
One does for Her *ka*,
Hethert, the Venerable,
Lady of Senmet.[68]

---

[68] Inconnu-Bocquillon, Danielle, *Le mythe de la déesse lointaine à Philae, BdE 132*, (Le Caire/Cairo: IFAO, 2001), 32-33.

HYMN OF HETHERT

Hethert, the Great, Mistress of Dendera
Eye of Ra, in the midst of...
Princess of All the Gods,
Who came out of the Primeval Waters
With the Creator of the World,
All the Gods came into being after their creation.
Noble, Mistress of Intoxication,
Mistress of Myrrh, Princess of Wreath-Making,
You use the *Shem*-Sistrum, the *Menit* and the *Sesheshet*-Sistrum
Hethert, the Great, Mistress of Dendera.[69]

---

[69] Kockelmann, Holger and Erich Winter, *Philae III: Die Zweite Ostkolonnade des Tempels der Isis in Philae. (CO II und CO II K)*, (Verlag der Österreichischen Akademie der Wissenschaften/Austrian Academy of Sciences, 2016), 20-21. Translated by Chelsea Bolton.

HYMN OF HETHERT

Great Falcon Goddess,
Mistress of the Lake of Flames,
Glorious, Great in Heaven and on Earth,
Uraeus Snake, Living One
With the Perfect Face
Loveliest in All the Lands,
Most Magnificent of the Magnificent
Strongest of the Strong
Queen of Upper and Lower Egypt
Hethert, the Great, Mistress of Senmet
Glorious, Powerful
Who came from Kenset,
She reaches Senmet as the Great Wepeset (Flame Goddess),
And makes a stop there with the flame around Her
Who sends the blaze of flame against Her enemy,
She is angry as Sekhmet and pacified as Bast,
Who makes the Two Lands thrive with Her Scepter of Life,
May She give Her popularity among the Nine Gods (Ennead) to the
    Son of Ra (Ptolemy VIII).[70]

---

[70] Kockelmann, Holger and Erich Winter, *Philae III: Die Zweite Ostkolonnade des Tempels der Isis in Philae. (CO II und CO II K)*, (Verlag der Osterreichischen Akademie der Wissenschaften/Austrian Academy of Sciences, 2016), 260-261. Translated by Chelsea Bolton.

Hymn of Hethert

Hethert, the Great,
Lady of Iunet, Eye of Ra,
Lady of Heaven, Mistress of All the Gods,
Seshat, the Great, Lady of the Library,
The gods rise in the morning in order to pay homage to Her.[71]

---

[71] Adapted from a translation by Barbara A. Richter in Richter, Barbara A., *The Theology of Hathor of Dendera: Aural and Visual Scribal Techniques in the Per-Wer Sanctuary*, (Lockwood Press, 2016), 302. Translated by Barbara A. Richter. Used with permission.

HYMN OF HETHERT

Hethert, Foremost One of Iunet,
Powerful One, Mistress of the Gods and Goddesses,
Great One of Heaven,
Female Ruler on Earth,
The gods rejoice for Her when She appears.[72]

---

[72] Adapted from a translation by Barbara A. Richter in Richter, Barbara A., *The Theology of Hathor of Dendera: Aural and Visual Scribal Techniques in the Per-Wer Sanctuary*, (Lockwood Press, 2016), 304. Translated by Barbara A. Richter. Used with permission.

HYMN OF HETHERT

Hethert, the Great,
Lady of Iunet, Eye of Ra
Lady of Heaven, Mistress of All the Gods.[73]

---

[73] Adapted from a translation by Barbara A. Richter in Richter, Barbara A., *The Theology of Hathor of Dendera: Aural and Visual Scribal Techniques in the Per-Wer Sanctuary*, (Lockwood Press, 2016), 308. Translated by Barbara A. Richter. Used with permission.

HYMN OF HETHERT

Hethert, the Great,
Lady of Iunet, Eye of Ra
Lady of Heaven, Mistress of All the Gods,
Great One of Love, Mistress of Women,
Beautiful One of face among the braided ones,
Noble and Great Lady,
Lady of the Great Ladies,
The Beautiful One is beautiful in seeing Her!
How joyful to see Her!
How sweet to follow Her!
How beautiful is what She places in the heart!
The Gods rejoice in Her,
The *Ihy*-children make music for Her!
The Goddesses are praising Her Ka,
The Great One of Heaven,
Who brightens the Two Lands with Her rays,
The *Atenet* who fills the land with gold dust.
Her father Ra—His arms are around Her Incarnation.
Tenen adorns Her with Her adornments.[74]

---

[74] Adapted from a translation by Barbara A. Richter in Richter, Barbara A., *The Theology of Hathor of Dendera: Aural and Visual Scribal Techniques in the Per-Wer Sanctuary*, (Lockwood Press, 2016), 315-316. Translated by Barbara A. Richter. Used with permission.

Hymn of Hethert

Adoration to You,
Golden One, Lady of Iunet
The Noble and Powerful Lady in the Sanctuary of the Noble Lady,
She Who shines like gold in the Temple of the Sistrum,
The *Atenet* in the Land of Atum,
I adore Your Incarnation with what Your heart desires,
I invoke Your statue with the sacred texts.
I exalt Your *ka* to the height of Heaven.
I praise Your statue to the extent of the rays of the Aten.
May You come in peace.
May You go in joy!
Sweet is Your heart in hearing the praises.
Hethert, the Great, Lady of Iunet,
Eye of Ra, Lady of Heaven,
Mistress of All the Gods,
The Great *Uraeus*, Lady of the *Per Wer*,
Your beautiful face is satisfied with Your beloved.[75]

---

[75] Adapted from a translation by Barbara A. Richter in Richter, Barbara A., *The Theology of Hathor of Dendera: Aural and Visual Scribal Techniques in the Per-Wer Sanctuary*, (Lockwood Press, 2016), 320. Translated by Barbara A. Richter. Used with permission.

HYMN OF HETHERT

Adoration to You
The *Atenet* in Tarer (Dendera),
The Noble One in the Palace of the Noble One,
The *Uraeus* of the Horizon-Dweller,
In the Sanctuary of the Golden One,
The Female Sovereign in *Iatdi*,
I exalt Your body in order to sweeten Your heart.
I make Your *Ba*-power greater than that of the Gods.
I invoke Your statues with the formulas of Sia
and with the magical utterances of Your manifestation.
May You come in joy.
May You walk in joy.
Your Incarnation is joyful in Your beauty/perfection.
Hethert, the Great, Lady of Iunet,
Eye of Ra, Lady of Heaven,
Mistress of All the Gods,
The Noble and Powerful Lady in the Temple of the Sistrum,
Your beautiful face is satisfied with Your beloved.[76]

---

[76] Adapted from a translation by Barbara A. Richter in Richter, Barbara A., *The Theology of Hathor of Dendera: Aural and Visual Scribal Techniques in the Per-Wer Sanctuary*, (Lockwood Press, 2016), 322. Translated by Barbara A. Richter. Used with permission.

HYMN OF HETHERT

Hethert, the Great, Lady of Iunet,
Eye of Ra, Lady of Heaven,
Mistress of All the Gods,
Lady of Drunkenness (or Beer),
Lady of Myrrh, Lady of Music,
Mistress, who ties the headband.[77]

---

[77] Adapted from a translation by Barbara A. Richter in Richter, Barbara A., *The Theology of Hathor of Dendera: Aural and Visual Scribal Techniques in the Per-Wer Sanctuary*, (Lockwood Press, 2016), 333-334. Translated by Barbara A. Richter. Used with permission.

HYMN OF HETHERT

I have played music before Your beautiful face,
Golden One,
I make calm Your heart with praises.
I have pacified Your *Ka* in the Sanctuary of the Noble Lady,
the *menit*-necklace, and the *sss.t*-sistrum in my hands,
for You are the Eye of Ra, Mistress of the Goddesses,
Who adorns the brow of Ra with beauty.[78]

---

[78] Adapted from a translation by Barbara A. Richter in Richter, Barbara A., *The Theology of Hathor of Dendera: Aural and Visual Scribal Techniques in the Per-Wer Sanctuary*, (Lockwood Press, 2016), 339. Translated by Barbara A. Richter. Used with permission.

HYMN OF HETHERT

I have praised Your *Ka* to the Height of Heaven,
I have kissed the ground for You to the extent of the breath of the
    earth,
I have greeted You,
My mouth possessing the prayers,
My heart possessing the utterances,
I praise Your Incarnation in Qabtawy,
Noble and Powerful Lady in the Temple of the Bier.[79]

---

[79] Adapted from a translation by Barbara A. Richter in Richter, Barbara A., *The Theology of Hathor of Dendera: Aural and Visual Scribal Techniques in the Per-Wer Sanctuary*, (Lockwood Press, 2016), 343. Translated by Barbara A. Richter. Used with permission.

HYMN OF HETHERT

Hethert, Lady of Iunet,
Eye of Ra, *Uraeus* of Ra in Iunet,
The Female Creator who was first to be born,
without another except for Her,
who nourishes Her child with Her white milk.[80]

---

[80] Adapted from a translation by Barbara A. Richter in Richter, Barbara A., *The Theology of Hathor of Dendera: Aural and Visual Scribal Techniques in the Per-Wer Sanctuary*, (Lockwood Press, 2016), 344. Translated by Barbara A. Richter. Used with permission.

HYMN OF HETHERT

Greetings to You,
Noble Lady, my Mistress,
Whose divine power is greater than that of all the gods,
You are called the Golden One,
Lady of Iunet, Lady of Protection,
Protecting the One who created Her.[81]

---

[81] Adapted from a translation by Barbara A. Richter in Richter, Barbara A., *The Theology of Hathor of Dendera: Aural and Visual Scribal Techniques in the Per-Wer Sanctuary*, (Lockwood Press, 2016), 345. Translated by Barbara A. Richter. Used with permission.

Hymn of Hethert

Hethert, the Great,
Lady of Iunet, Eye of Ra,
She who is Highest of the Great Seat,
Lady of Heaven, Mistress of All the Gods,
The First Daughter of Her Father Ra,
Who hears the prayers of everyone.[82]

---

[82] Adapted from a translation by Barbara A. Richter in Richter, Barbara A., *The Theology of Hathor of Dendera: Aural and Visual Scribal Techniques in the Per-Wer Sanctuary*, (Lockwood Press, 2016), 345. Translated by Barbara A. Richter. Used with permission.

HYMN OF HETHERT

Hethert, Lady of Iunet,
The *Menit*, Eye of Ra,
The Beautiful One in all Her names,
The Shining and Powerful One,
The Protectress for Her brother,
Who makes his protection against his enemies.[83]

---

[83] Adapted from a translation by Barbara A. Richter in Richter, Barbara A., *The Theology of Hathor of Dendera: Aural and Visual Scribal Techniques in the Per-Wer Sanctuary*, (Lockwood Press, 2016), 360. Translated by Barbara A. Richter. Used with permission.

HYMN OF HETHERT

Hethert, Lady of Iunet,
Eye of Ra, Lady of Heaven,
Mistress of All the Gods,
She who takes the inventory,
Lady of Protection,
She has united with the *Uraeus* on the Head of Her Father.[84]

---

[84] Adapted from a translation by Barbara A. Richter in Richter, Barbara A., *The Theology of Hathor of Dendera: Aural and Visual Scribal Techniques in the Per-Wer Sanctuary*, (Lockwood Press, 2016), 362. Translated by Barbara A. Richter. Used with permission.

Hymn of the Uraeus

The *Uraeus* is within the Temple of the *Wensheb*,
Bright One of face in Her sanctuary that She loves,
Uniting with the Left Eye, brightening the Banks,
Leading the Two Lands with Her beauties,
For She is Lady of Life, the Sweet One of Love,
Who illuminates this land with Her shining Eyes.[85]

---

[85] Adapted from a translation by Barbara A. Richter in Richter, Barbara A., *The Theology of Hathor of Dendera: Aural and Visual Scribal Techniques in the Per-Wer Sanctuary*, (Lockwood Press, 2016), 362. Translated by Barbara A. Richter. Used with permission.

Hymn of Hethert

Hethert, the Great, Lady of Iunet,
Eye of Ra, Lady of Heaven,
Mistress of All the Gods,
She who does not have Her equal in Heaven and on Earth,
Great One of Love, Mistress of Women,
Lady of the *sss.t*-Sistrum,
Lady of the *shm*-Sistra,
Lady of Music, Lady of Gladness,
Lady of Jubilation, Lady of Joy,
Mistress of the *ib3*-Dance,
Lady of Myrrh,
Who ties the headband.[86]

---

[86] Adapted from a translation by Barbara A. Richter in Richter, Barbara A., *The Theology of Hathor of Dendera: Aural and Visual Scribal Techniques in the Per-Wer Sanctuary*, (Lockwood Press, 2016), 365. Translated by Barbara A. Richter. Used with permission.

HYMN OF HETHERT

The Lady of Iunet is satisfied/rests in Iunet
as the Lady of the *sss.t*-sistrum,
Mistress of the *shm*-sistra,
Driving away anger, dispelling rage,
Destroying evil in front of Her face,
For She is the Bright One of face,
The Sweet One of Love,
Her Father is satisfied in seeing Her.[87]

---

[87] Adapted from a translation by Barbara A. Richter in Richter, Barbara A., *The Theology of Hathor of Dendera: Aural and Visual Scribal Techniques in the Per-Wer Sanctuary*, (Lockwood Press, 2016), 365. Translated by Barbara A. Richter. Used with permission.

HYMN OF HETHERT

The Female King of Upper and Lower Egypt,
Female Ruler in Kab-Tawy (Dendera),
The Beautiful One of Face,
Festive One of Eyes,
Noble and Powerful Lady,
There is no knowing Her body,
The Sacred One among the Ennead,
Who rests in Her shrine in Her sacred sanctuary.
Hethert, the Great, Lady of Iunet.[88]

---

[88] Adapted from a translation by Barbara A. Richter in Richter, Barbara A., *The Theology of Hathor of Dendera: Aural and Visual Scribal Techniques in the Per-Wer Sanctuary*, (Lockwood Press, 2016), 370. Translated by Barbara A. Richter. Used with permission.

HYMN OF HETHERT

Hethert, the Great,
Lady of Iunet, Eye of Ra,
Mistress of All the Gods,
Noble and Great Lady,
Mistress of the God's Land (Dendera)
Who follows Her heart in the Valley of Myrrh
Pleasant One of Perfume, Sweet One of Love,
She unites with the fragrance of Her chapel,
Ma'at the Great, Bright One of Appearance,
The *Atenet*, who shoots forth rays like Her father Ra.
The Eye of Ra, Who shines in Heaven,
Illuminating the Sky and Land with Her beauty,
Giving joy, Dispelling sadness,
Protecting Her father from the enemy.
For She is the Female Falcon,
The Dappled One of Plumage,
Behdetyt~She Who comes from Behdet,
Lady of Punt.[89]

---

[89] Adapted from a translation by Barbara A. Richter in Richter, Barbara A., *The Theology of Hathor of Dendera: Aural and Visual Scribal Techniques in the Per-Wer Sanctuary*, (Lockwood Press, 2016), 387-388. Translated by Barbara A. Richter. Used with permission. I put here *Behdetyt* means "She Who Comes from Behdet". Richter has this as *Behdetyt* here. I changed it so the meaning of the word is within the hymn to make it more clear.

HYMN OF HETHERT

Hail, Eye of Ra
Whose manifestations are numerous,
Lady of Names throughout the Two Lands,
Bright One of brightness among the Gods,
One does not know Her statue.
Secret One of Form, Hidden One of Image,
Powerful One of *Ba*-power for Her father,
Great One in Heaven,
who brightens the Two Lands with Her beauties,
the Goddess who does not have Her equal,
Lady of Love, one rejoices at seeing Her.
The Gods rejoice at seeing Her,
Luminous One in the Horizon,
Who illuminates the Two Lands with Her rays,
The *Atenet*, First Daughter of the Aten,
Beautiful Noblewoman, without another except for Her,
Without Her likeness among the Goddesses,
The very Beautiful One,
Beautiful One in Appearance in Netjeryt,
Hethert, the Great,
Lady of Iunet,
Your beautiful face is satisfied.[90]

---

[90] Adapted from a translation by Barbara A. Richter in Richter, Barbara A., *The Theology of Hathor of Dendera: Aural and Visual Scribal Techniques in the Per-Wer Sanctuary*, (Lockwood Press, 2016), 409-410. Translated by Barbara A. Richter. Used with permission.

HYMNS OF MENHYT

HYMN OF MENHYT

You are Raet, who illuminates the Two Lands:
She abides and streams with light on the head of Ra, in this Her
    name of Menhyt,
You are the extent of the water, who did what is,
Created beings, Mother of God,
Who created the Gods,
Menhyt—both wind and flood—
Great Mother, who begins to create fertile grain,
Who made the surface of the water
And created everything in Your name of Nit.

You are the sacred and powerful Goddess,
Whom Ra is delighted to see,
Great of Love, Bast,
Great Goddess of the Festival,
In whose favor we begin to play the tambourine,
Pupil of the Solar Eye,
Mother of God, Mother of Creation,
in this Your name of Mut.

You are the daughter for whom Her father Ra has seen the horizon,
The throne, the scepter and Her royalty are on the Sky and on the
    Earth
So that She is satisfied with it,
In this Your name of Nebet Hetepet.

You are the Great of Magic, the Almighty of the Ennead,
Lady of Respect, Mistress of the Day and Month,

In favor of whom one makes an annual feast,
In order to appease Her,
In this Your name of Sekhmet.

You are the eminent Lady of the Gods and Goddesses,
Uraeus, who stands on the head of Your Father Ra,
In Your name of Mehyt.

You are the Mistress of Agny,
Who goes up to Thebes as Mafdet,
Who puts Shu in the world in the Temple of Mut,
Eye of Ra, who enters the Nome of Heliopolis
At the Feast of the Sixth Day,
In this Your name of Hethert.
You are the Cobra of Life,
Lady of the Palace,
Mistress of Heaven,
Guide of the Two Lands,
Great of Counsel
In every place,
In this Your name of Aset.

You are the one who presides over the marshes,
Serpent of Life in the Sky,
Who causes the enthronement of the Phoenix,
And brings out the flood of the Two Caverns,
To flood the Two Lands in Her season,
In this Your name of Sopdet.

You are the Golden One,
Lady of the Countryside,
Renenutet, Wadjet,
Who gives birth to everything where She goes,

Beneficent One, who organizes the nomes and cities
Through what She has created
In this Your name of Nebetuu.
May Your beautiful face be gracious.[91]

---

[91] Sauneron, Serge, *Esna V: Les fêtes religieuses d'Esna aux derniers siècles du paganisme*, (Cairo: IFAO, 1962; 2004), 107-108. Translated by Chelsea Bolton. Thank you to Edward P. Butler for his help with this translation.

HYMNS OF MUT

HYMN OF MUT

Mut, Mistress of *Isheru*
Mistress of Heaven
Queen of All the Gods.[92]

---

[92] Breasted, James Henry, *Ancient Records of Egypt: The Nineteenth Dynasty Volume III*, (Chicago: University of Chicago Press, 1906), 69. Translated by James Henry Breasted.

HYMN OF MUT

Mut, Venerable, Mistress of *Isheru*
Lady of Senmet, Eye of Ra
She Who is at the head of Ta-Sety,
Uraeus, on the Head of Her Father,
She Who throws Her fiery breath against Her enemies,
She Who slaughters Apep daily.[93]

---

[93] Inconnu-Bocquillon, Danielle, *Le mythe de la déesse lointaine à Philae, BdE 132*, (Le Caire/Cairo: IFAO, 2001), 23.

HYMN OF MUT

Mut, Venerable
Mistress of *Isheru*,
Eye of Ra, Mistress of the Sky,
Regent and Lady, Who resides in the Abaton,
Lady of Philae, *Uraeus* on the Head of Her Father.[94]

---

[94] Inconnu-Bocquillon, Danielle, *Le mythe de la déesse lointaine à Philae, BdE 132*, (Le Caire/Cairo: IFAO, 2001), 26.

HYMN OF MUT

Mut, Venerable, Mistress of *Isheru*,
Tefnut, Daughter of Ra,
Who resides in the Abaton,
August and Powerful,
Regent of the Goddesses,
On the Head of Her Father,
She Who comes from Kenset and goes to Senmet,
She Who sits there, preferably to any other place.[95]

---

[95] Inconnu-Bocquillon, Danielle, *Le mythe de la déesse lointaine à Philae, BdE 132*, (Le Caire/Cairo: IFAO, 2001), 42.

HYMN OF MUT

Mut, Venerable, Mistress of *Isheru*,
August and Perfect in Senmet,
Eye of Ra, Mistress of the Sky,
Regent of All the Gods,
Wepeset,
Venerable in the Palace of Flame,
Female Ra,
Regent of Kenset, Mafdet in Bugem.[96]

---

[96] Inconnu-Bocquillon, Danielle, *Le mythe de la déesse lointaine à Philae, BdE 132*, (Le Caire/Cairo: IFAO, 2001), 46.

HYMN OF MUT

Mut, Eye of Ra,
Who illuminates the Two Lands,
Mut, Eye of Ra,
Mistress of the Sky,
Regent of All the Gods,
Mut, Venerable,
Lady of *Isheru*,
Eye of Ra,
Mistress of the Sky,
Regent of All the Gods.[97]

---

[97] Inconnu-Bocquillon, Danielle, *Le mythe de la déesse lointaine à Philae, BdE 132*, (Le Caire/Cairo: IFAO, 2001), 47.

HYMN OF MUT

Mut, Venerable,
Mistress of *Isheru*,
Eye of Ra
Who resides in the Abaton,
Who is at the Head of Philae.[98]

---

[98] Inconnu-Bocquillon, Danielle, *Le mythe de la déesse lointaine à Philae*, BdE 132, (Le Caire/Cairo: IFAO, 2001), 52.

Hymn of Mut

Mut, Venerable, Mistress of *Isheru*
Eye of Ra, Mistress of the Sky,
Regent of All the Gods,
Lady of Karnak,
Divine Mother of Khonsu, the Child.[99]

---

[99] Inconnu-Bocquillon, Danielle, *Le mythe de la déesse lointaine à Philae, BdE 132*, (Le Caire/Cairo: IFAO, 2001), 69.

HYMN OF MUT

Mut, Venerable,
Mistress of *Isheru*,
Eye of Ra,
Mistress of the Sky,
One at the head of Senmet.[100]

---

[100] Inconnu-Bocquillon, Danielle, *Le mythe de la déesse lointaine à Philae, BdE 132*, (Le Caire/Cairo: IFAO, 2001), 76.

HYMN OF MUT

Mut, Venerable,
Mistress of *Isheru*,
August and Powerful,
Regent in the Palace of the Front,
Uraeus,
Venerable,
on the Head of the Chapel of God,
She Who refreshes Her ardor in the Abaton,
She Who comes from Ta-Sety,
Her brother Shu adores Her.[101]

---

[101] Inconnu-Bocquillon, Danielle, *Le mythe de la déesse lointaine à Philae, BdE 132*, (Le Caire/Cairo: IFAO, 2001), 81.

HYMN OF MUT

Mut, Venerable,
Mistress of *Isheru*,
Eye of Ra,
Mistress of Heaven,
Regent of All the Gods.[102]

---

[102] Inconnu-Bocquillon, Danielle, *Le mythe de la déesse lointaine à Philae*, BdE 132, (Le Caire/Cairo: IFAO, 2001), 119.

HYMN TO MUT

Mut, the Great
Mistress of *Isheru*,
Mother of the God Heru, the Strong Bull
Glorious One, Powerful One,
Who is without equal,
Mut, the Great,
Mistress of *Isheru*.[103]

---

[103] Kockelmann, Holger and Erich Winter, *Philae III: Die Zweite Ostkolonnade des Tempels der Isis in Philae. (CO II und CO II K)*, (Verlag der Osterreichischen Akademie der Wissenschaften/Austrian Academy of Sciences, 2016), 46. Translated by Chelsea Bolton. I changed Horus to his ancient Egyptian name Heru.

Hymn of Mut

Mut, Great of *Isheru*,
Eye of Ra,
Mistress of the Sky,
Princess of All the Gods,
Mistress of Karnak,
Mother of Khonsu, the Child.[104]

---

[104] Kockelmann, Holger and Erich Winter, *Philae III: Die Zweite Ostkolonnade des Tempels der Isis in Philae. (CO II und CO II K)*, (Verlag der Österreichischen Akademie der Wissenschaften/Austrian Academy of Sciences, 2016), 180. Translated by Chelsea Bolton.

Hymn of Mut

Mut, the Great,
Mistress of *Isheru*
Eye of Ra,
Mistress of Heaven,
Princess of Senmet.
Glorious One, Powerful One,
Who overshadows the Gods.[105]

---

[105] Kockelmann, Holger and Erich Winter, *Philae III: Die Zweite Ostkolonnade des Tempels der Isis in Philae. (CO II und CO II K)*, (Verlag der Osterreichischen Akademie der Wissenschaften/Austrian Academy of Sciences, 2016), 224. Translated by Chelsea Bolton.

HYMN OF MUT

Mut, the Great,
Mistress of *Isheru*
Eye of Ra,
Mistress of the Sky
At the Head of Senmet.[106]

---

[106] Kockelmann, Holger and Erich Winter, *Philae III: Die Zweite Ostkolonnade des Tempels der Isis in Philae. (CO II und CO II K)*, (Verlag der Osterreichischen Akademie der Wissenschaften/Austrian Academy of Sciences, 2016), 297. Translated by Chelsea Bolton.

HYMN OF MUT

Mut, the Lady of *Isheru*,
The Lady of the Sky,
The Mistress of the Gods,
Who Protects Her City,
The Mistress of Power,
Bold One, Powerful of Heart,
Sekhmet-Bast-Wadjet,
The First of Atum,
Who Strews the Two Lands
With the Electrum of Her Face.[107]

---

[107] Bryan, Betsy M. "Hatshepsut and Cultic Revelries in the New Kingdom." *Creativity and Innovation in the Reign of Hatshepsut*, SAOC 69 (2014): 101. Translated by Betsy M. Bryan.

HYMN OF MUT

Mut, the Great,
Lady of the *Isheru*-lake,
Eye of Ra, Lady of Heaven,
Mistress of All the Gods,
Noble and Powerful Lady in the Sanctuary of the Noble Lady,
Who floods the sanctuary of the Golden One with joy.[108]

---

[108] Adapted from a translation by Barbara A. Richter in Richter, Barbara A., *The Theology of Hathor of Dendera: Aural and Visual Scribal Techniques in the Per-Wer Sanctuary*, (Lockwood Press, 2016), 353. Translated by Barbara A. Richter. Used with permission.

NEW YEAR'S HYMN OF MUT AS SEKHMET-BAST-MUT

Good Mother, be good to me.
Mother of the victory chant,
The victory of Heru-sema-tawy the child,
Great Ihy, Hethert's son;
My life shines for You.
Foremost Mother, be foremost for me,
And I will be powerful in my shining years.
Healthy Mother, be healthy for me, make me endure.
May Your beginning be life, Your middle health,
and Your end prosperity.
Protect me against all enemies, dead or alive.
Peaceful Mother, come in peace.
Give Your favor to the Great and Lesser Nine;
Give Your favor to *akhu* and men.
O Pure Mother, be pure for me,
In every difficulty and challenge this year.[109]

---

[109] Siuda, Tamara L., The *Ancient Egyptian Prayerbook*, (Illinois: Stargazer Design, 2009), 71. Translated by Tamara L. Siuda.

HYMNS OF NEBET HET

(Nebt-Het; Nephthys)

HYMN OF NEBET HET

Nebet Het, Sister of the Gods,
Lady of Senmet,
Venerable and Perfect at the Head of Philae,
Excellent Sovereign, Regent of the Goddesses,
One Who Makes the anger of the Gods disappear for Her brother
As long as *Kherseket* is appeased in the Abaton,
To ensure the protection of Her brother,
To grow Her prestige in the face of His enemies,
To inspire fear in His adversaries,
She is the *Qerhet* (Most Noble Goddess),
Who stands on Her tail
To send the burning breath
against the enemies of Wesir.[110]

---

[110] Inconnu-Bocquillon, Danielle, *Le mythe de la déesse lointaine à Philae*, BdE 132, (Le Caire/Cairo: IFAO, 2001), 37. Thank you to Tamara L. Siuda, Edward Butler and Astrid Tanebet for their help with this translation. Thank you to Tamara L. Siuda for her help with this translation. Qerhet means "Most Noble Goddess" and can also be a Cobra form as an Eye of Ra.

HYMN OF NEBET HET

Nebet Het, Sister of God,
Mistress of the Palace
One who sends the flame
against the enemies of Her brother.[111]

---

[111] Inconnu-Bocquillon, Danielle, *Le mythe de la déesse lointaine à Philae, BdE 132*, (Le Caire/Cairo: IFAO, 2001), 80.

Hymn of Nebet Het

Nebet Het, the Great,
Sister of God,
Who resides in the Abaton,
Flame,
Who burns the enemies,
Perfect Sovereign,
Whose likeness does not exist,
One Who Protects Her brother in the Cities and Nomes,
As long as the August and Powerful One
is the One Who appears in Philae,
Excellent Goddess, Without Equal,
To receive the Two Jugs of the Two Ladies,
To drink the beer,
Joyful is Her Heart with Her words,
She is the Great Sovereign,
She Who watches over Her brother Wesir,
And protects His body in the Abaton.[112]

---

[112] Inconnu-Bocquillon, Danielle, *Le mythe de la déesse lointaine à Philae, BdE 132*, (Le Caire/Cairo: IFAO, 2001), 89. Thank you to Tamara L. Siuda for her help with this translation.

HYMN OF NEBET HET

Nebet Het, Sister of God in the midst of Philae,
Excellent Goddess of Her sister Aset.
Nebet Het says:
The Powerful One, Who Gives...
To this one (the King),
Who protects the son of Wesir
and keeps his body safe
Nebet Het, the Excellent One.[113]

---

[113] Kockelmann, Holger and Erich Winter, *Philae III: Die Zweite Ostkolonnade des Tempels der Isis in Philae. (CO II und CO II K)*, (Verlag der Österreichischen Akademie der Wissenschaften/Austrian Academy of Sciences, 2016), 28-29. Translated by Chelsea Bolton. I changed Nephthys to her ancient Egyptian name Nebt Het. I changed Osiris to his ancient Egyptian name Wesir. Thank you to Tamara L. Siuda, Astrid Tanebet and Carissa D. for their help with this translation.

HYMN OF NEBET HET

Nebet Het,
Excellent of the Gods,
Sister of God,
Lady of Senmet.[114]

---

[114] Kockelmann, Holger and Erich Winter, *Philae III: Die Zweite Ostkolonnade des Tempels der Isis in Philae. (CO II und CO II K)*, (Verlag der Osterreichischen Akademie der Wissenschaften/Austrian Academy of Sciences, 2016), 291. Translated by Chelsea Bolton. I changed Nephthys to her ancient Egyptian name Nebt Het. I changed Osiris to his ancient Egyptian name Wesir.

HYMN OF NEBET HET

Nebet Het, in the midst of Philae,
Sister of Her brother Wesir.[115]

---

[115] Kockelmann, Holger and Erich Winter, *Philae III: Die Zweite Ostkolonnade des Tempels der Isis in Philae. (CO II und CO II K)*, (Verlag der Osterreichischen Akademie der Wissenschaften/Austrian Academy of Sciences, 2016), 161. Translated by Chelsea Bolton. I changed Nephthys to her ancient Egyptian name Nebet Het. I changed Osiris to his ancient Egyptian name Wesir.

HYMN OF NEBET HET

Nebet Het, Sister of God in Edfu,
Effective One, Young One,
Who is Great in Edfu,
One with the Beautiful Face,
the Bright Eyes,
Kind and Full of Love.[116]

---

[116] Bergman, Jan. "Nephthys découverte dans un papyrus magique". *Melanges Adolphe Gutbub.* (Institut d'égyptologie, Université Paul Valéry, 1984), pp. 7. Temple of Edfu

HYMN OF NEBET HET

Accountant of the Time of Life,
Mistress of the Years,
Mistress of Shai and Reret,
Sun Goddess,
Who decides existence
And makes the perfect condition of Wennefer, True of Voice.[117]

---

[117] Bergman, Jan. "Nephthys découverte dans un papyrus magique". *Melanges Adolphe Gutbub*. (Institut d'égyptologie, Université Paul Valéry, 1984), pp. 6. Temple of Dendera

HYMN OF NEBET HET

Nebet Het, the Excellent,
Who resides in *Iatdi*,
the Protector of Her brother,
Who protects His Majesty
in the Necropolis of the country.[118]

---

[118] Cauville, Sylvie, *Le Temple de Dendera: La Porte d'Isis, Dendara,* (Cairo: IFAO, 1999), 96-97.
    Translated by Chelsea Bolton. I changed Nephthys to the ancient Egyptian name Nebet Het.

HYMN OF NEBET HET

To Make Adoration to His Mother, the Very Great,
Who loves Her brother Wesir,
Mother of the son whom She loves,
Adoration to Your beautiful face
Nebet Het, the Great,
Mistress of the District of the Gazelle,
Purifier, Radiant One,
Who presides in Pi-Khnum.
The Great, Excellent One,
Residing in the Beautiful West
The dwelling of Her brother Wesir, Who comes to life again in
    Her,
She who renews for Him the body of this One
in Her Name of Renewal of Life,
of Youth,
Guardian of the Wellbeing of the God for the *Ka* of this One
Adoration to You, *Kherseket*, the Great
Daughter of Ra, Who has united with Ma'at the Great,
Beloved of Khnum, Female Ra,
Mistress of the Two Lands, Venerable Mistress of the Two Lands,
Great Lady of the House of Amun.
Beautiful of Face, Whose Two Eyes are painted for the
    Festival...Exactly.
To You, Meskhenet, the Excellent,
Who gives life to the Two Lands and
gives the breath of air to all nostrils,
Praise to You, the Beautiful One, on all the submerged lands,
Who floods the Two Lands with Barley and Wheat for His *Ka*

To You, the Mistress of Drunkenness,
To the Numerous Festivals,
Mistress of Joy, Lady of Dance,
To You, Mistress of Beer,
Who loves the Day of the Festival,
For whom the men and women play the tambourine.
To You, Tefnut, when She has become angry,
Who can support His need?
To You, Mother of Heru, Divine Wife of Wennefer, the justified,
The Most Excellent,
Beautiful One, Who preserves Heru and Wesir.
To You, Seshat the Great, Mistress of Men,
Mistress of Writing, Lady of the Entire Library,
To You, Who commands the divine decrees
Great of Magic,
Who resides in the House of the Archivists.
To You, Mistress of Renewal,
Who began to mark the enemies of the divine slaughter
To You, Great of Magic, Excellent of Kindness,
Who created the Ennead, according to what She ordered,
To You, *Merkhetes*, the Dreaded,
Nebet Het, the Divine Sister,
Who protects Her brother in the flood
To You, Opet, on the Head of Her Father,
Great Venerable One in the Arms of the *Heh*-Spirits,
To You, Meret of the North,
Who guards the members of the God in the Palace of Gold,
in His time,
To You, Khenemty, the Powerful One,
Who presides over the Souls of Heliopolis.
Hekat in the Island of Fire,
To You, Menhyt-Sekhmet of Esna,
Nebetuu-Tefnut in the Countryside of Khnum

To You, Great Mother of Amun,
Daughter of Ra, Who loves His *Ka*,
Of the Place of Her Power in the Two Lands.
To You, Nehemet-away, Wenut of the South,
Hekat, who announces events,
To You, Meret of the South, Wenut of the North,
Eye of Ra, Mistress of Beauty
Who shines before Ra,
To You, Sovereign of All Men,
Who vivifies Human Beings
Mistress of the Fresh Skin (python-skin),
To You, Khensut, on the Head of Soped,
Kind One, Excellent Advisor of the Soul of the East,
To You, Mut, Mistress of Humans,
Who protects the Gods,
Mafdet, go forth...Divine,
To Hethert, the *Akhet* Cow in any district,
Mistress of Drunkenness, Who created the beer *Wnw*,
Come in Peace, Attentive One,
Honorable of Face,
I make for You the gifts which are appropriate,
In Kindness
I exalt Your power,
As the desire of the One Whose Two Feminine Attributes are
    Beautiful,
I am Your son, whom you love and who is on the throne of
    eternity.
Words Spoken by Nebet Het, the Great, Who loves Her brother,
Whose names are numerous in all the cities,
Men and Women halt before Your residence
To make adoration to Your *Ka*![119]

---

[119] El-Saghir, Mohamed and Dominique Valbelle. "Komir. I. - The Discovery of Komir Temple.
    Preliminary Report. II. - Deux hymnes aux divinites de Komir : Anoukis et Nephthys." *BIFAO 83*

DAWN PRAYER: PYRAMID TEXTS: SPELL 216

I have come to You, Nebet Het,
I have come to You, Night-boat,
I have come to You, True-Before-Dawn,
I have come to You, birth-brick of souls,
Remember me.
It is well with me and with You,
It is peaceful for me and for You,
Within the arms of Our Father,
Within the arms of Atum.[120]

(1983), p. 164-166. Translated by Chelsea Bolton. Thank you to Edward Butler and Tamara L. Siuda for their help with this translation. Hehous or the Heh Gods are the Eight pillars which hold up the sky. From the Temple of Komir.

[120] Siuda, Tamara L., The *Ancient Egyptian Prayerbook*, (Stargazer Design, 2009), 122-123. Translated by Tamara L. Siuda.

PYRAMID TEXTS: SPELL 364

Nebet Het,
collects all your members for you
in Her name of Seshat, Lady of Builders.[121]

---

[121] Siuda, Tamara L., *Nebt Het: Lady of the House*, (Stargazer Design, 2010), 11. Spell 364. Translated by
Tamara L. Siuda.

COFFIN TEXTS: SPELL 778

O (Name of Deceased Person),
Heru protects you,
He causes Nebet Het to hold you together,
To create you in Her Name of Seshat, Mistress of Potters
She is a Great Lady, Great of Life in the Night-boat,
Who raises Heru up.[122]

---

[122] Siuda, Tamara L., The *Ancient Egyptian Prayerbook*, (Stargazer Design, 2009), 73. Translated by Tamara L. Siuda.

HYMN FROM CANOPIC CHEST FROM THE SAITE PERIOD

Nebet Het, the Great,
Mistress of Women,
Sopdet,
Lady of Life of the Two Lands,
Mistress of the Eye of Light,
Luminous Pupils of the Two Sacred Eyes.[123]

---

[123] Bunsen, Christian Karl Josias, and Samuel Birch. *Egypt's place in universal history: an historical investigation in five books. Vol. 1*, (Longman, Brown, Green, and Longmans, 1848), 435. Arundale, Francis, and Joseph Bonomi, *Gallery of antiquities selected from the British Museum*, (J. Weale, 1842), 35. Translated by Tamara L. Siuda. British Museum: Museum Number: EA8539.

BROOKLYN MUSEUM PAPYRUS 47.218.50

Nebet Het, the Sister of God
Nebet Het, Who records the decrees of the Gods
Nebet Het, the most Powerful of the Two Goddesses
Nebet Het, the boat of the day.[124]

---

[124] Goyon, J.-Cl. *Confirmation du pouvoir royal au Nouvel An: Brooklyn Museum Papyrus 47.218.50, BdE 52*, (Cairo: IFAO, 1972), 66. Translated by Chelsea Bolton.

HYMN FROM CANOPIC BOX OF NS-'3-RWD (BM EA 8539)

Nebet Het, the Great, Mistress of Women
Sopdet, Lady of Ankhtawy
Lady of the Two Eyes,
Shining of Eyes, Sharp of Knife
Enduring of Body, Lady of Red Linen
Mistress of Green Linen, Beautiful One of the Divine Bark
Lady of Grace, Enduring of Love
Who encircles every heart in perfection
Braided One in the midst of the Great Temple
Sailor in the Great Sacred Bark.[125]

[125] Ouda, Ahmed M. Mekawy. "The Canopic Box of NS-'3-RWD (BM EA 8539)." *The Journal of Egyptian Archaeology 98, no. 1* (2012): 137. I changed Nephthys to her ancient Egyptian name Nebet Het.

LAMENTATIONS OF ASET AND NEBET HET

Aset:

Beautiful youth, come to Your house now; we cannot see You.

Hail beautiful boy, come to Your house, draw near after separation.

Hail beautiful youth, navigator of time, Who grows except now.

Holy image of His Father Tatenen, secret essence of Atum.

Nebet Het:

Lord, Lord! Much more wonderful than His Father,

Firstborn of His Mother.

Come to us bodily; we will embrace You.

Do not take Your beautiful face from us, clearly beloved.

Image of Tatnenen,

Master of love's joys, come in peace,

Lord we want to see You.

Aset:

Your Two Sisters reattach Your limbs,

no pain shall touch You.

We will make Your injuries as if they never happened.

Mighy One of the Gods,

the road You travel cannot be described.

Little One, child at morning and evening,

except when You circle Nut and Geb,

as the Bull of the Two Sisters.

Nebet Het:

Come, little one, growing young as You set.

Lord, we want to see You.

Come in peace, great child of His Father,
You are established in Your house.
Do not fear. Your son Heru avenges You.
Neka is carried off and thrust into his cave of fire every day;
his name hacked to pieces among all gods.
Tebha has become a stinking corpse.
You are in Your house, do not fear.
Apep suffers all the evil he committed.
What Nut sent him speared him.

Aset:
Come, youth of saffron face, growing young,
Whose two eyes are beautiful.
I am Your sister Aset, dear one of Your heart.
Because I love You and yet You are gone,
I water the earth with my tears.
While You travel, we sing,
And life springs up from Your absence.

Nebet Het:
O Lord, come in peace. Let us see You.
Hail prince, come in peace,
Drive away the fire in our houses.
Hail, bull of the Westerners, immovable,
How much more marvelous than the gods
Is the little one, the male,
The mighty heir of Geb, God among gods.

Aset:
Come to Your two widows;
The whole company of gods encircles You
That They may repel Apep, cursed be his name!
When he comes to the shrine before Your father

Ra Who shoots out fire and repels his devils.
Come, Your family waits.
Drive sorrow from our houses.
Come, Your family waits.
There is no one more stable than You, Who dwell alone.

Nebet Het:
Our Lord's throne is in peace.
Victor, greater than his suffering,
When the fiend lands on his enemies.
O born-again Soul,
The Two Sisters attach Your limbs.

Aset:
I hid myself in bushes to hide Your son,
that He might answer for You,
for Your death was a time of distress.
Didn't I collect Your limbs?
I went alone~I crept through the fields.
A large crocodile came after Your son,
a female crocodile with a male's face.
But I knew,
and Yinepu and I went around and retraced our steps
for my brother, keeping clear of evil.

Nebet Het:
Hail beautiful boy, come to Your exalted house.
Put Your back to it.
The gods are on their thrones.
Hail, come in peace, O King.

Aset:
Come in peace. Your son Heru avenges You.

You have caused grief to Your two queens.
And we weep at Your shrines.
Little One! How lovely it is to see You.
Come, come to us, Great One, glorify our love.
Come to Your house, do not be afraid.

Both (take turns):
O you gods in Heaven,
O you gods on earth,
O you gods in the Duat,
O you gods in the Abyss
O you gods in the service of Nun,
We follow the lord of love.

Aset:
I walk the roads so that Your love may find me.
I fly over Geb, I do not rest seeking You.

Nebet Het:
Your love is a flame,
Your body's scent like the perfume of Punt.
The Cow cries for You with Her voice.
She avenges You,
sets Your nose on Your face, collects Your bones.
Your Mother Nut comes to You with offerings.
She builds You up with the life of Her body.
You are granted a *ba* and a *ka*. You are established.

Aset:
You are established.
Your hair is turquoise on Your body,
Your hair is lapis;
Your hair and limbs are southern alabaster.

Your bones are silver,
Your teeth are turquoise,
the ointment of Your hair is liquid myrrh.
Your skull is lapis.

Both (take turns):
O you gods in Heaven,
O you gods on earth,
O you gods in the Duat,
O you gods in the Abyss
O you gods in the service of Nun,
We follow the lord of love.[126]

---

[126] Siuda, Tamara L., The *Ancient Egyptian Prayerbook*, (Illinois: Stargazer Design, 2009), 118-122. Translated by Tamara L. Siuda.

Birthday Prayer of Nebet Het

Light a candle for Nebt-het and pray:

O Nebt-het, Daughter of Nut, Sister of Set.
She Whose Father sees a healthy daughter
Stable of Face, Stable of Face,
I am the divine power in the womb of Her Mother, Nut.
Nebet Het, Daughter of Nut,
Save me from
any bad thing of this year,
from any slaughter of this year,
just as You have made my protection.
Protect me again, in the name of this day,
Child-Who-Is-In-His-Nest.[127]

---

[127] Siuda, Tamara L., *The Ancient Egyptian Daybook*, (Stargazer Design, 2016), 301. Translated by Tamara L. Siuda.

HYMNS OF NIT

(Net; Neith)

HYMN OF NIT

Adore Nit
Saying:

You are the Mistress of Sais,
That is the Primordial Mound (Tanen)
Whose Two-Thirds are Male and One-Third Female,
Primordial Goddess, Mysterious and Great,
Who began to be at the Beginning
And initiated everything;

You are the celestial vault,
In which...
She who gave birth to all the stars as they are,
And raised them on their chapels;
Whose breath burns the earth from flame of Her Eyes,
From the heat of Her mouth;
Divine Mother of Ra, Who shines on the horizon,
Mysterious One, Who shines with Her own light,

You are the Serpent Goddess,
Who came before them all,
Protector of the Whole Country,
Who began to be before those who were to be;
One under Her authority

You are the one who made the Underworld
In Her form of the Goddess,
Who touches to the limits of the Universe

In Her material form of the watery surface,
In Her name limitless duration.
Mistress of the Anointing Oil,
As well as pieces of clothing,
Goddess,
Who divided the comb of Her trade among the Five,
Inhabiting Heaven and Earth

You are the expanse of water,
Who created Tatenen, the God of the Primordial Mound
and Who created Nun
of Childbirth, from whom everything emerged;
Who makes the flood come out in its time
And who gives new youthfulness to the Water of Renewal in its
     season;
Who grows vegetation
Who creates the Tree of Life for the Living,
Who raises Nun......Mehet Weret ......one who rebels,

You are the Mistress of Esna,
In the mysterious countryside,
North of the Mound of the Two Birds,
One who suckles the Two Crocodiles
In their names of Shu and Tefnut
Guardian of Her Palaces,
Who embraces the neck of the Two Crocodiles in Her arms
That is Ra and Wesir,
The Two Birds,
Children of Her son Ra in Pi-Sahoure,
And Who provides the divine offerings of the Gods and
     Goddesses,

You are the Cow,

Lady of Khent-to,
Mistress of the Country of Ra,
In the Heart of the Mound of the Two Birds,
She Who supports the Sky on Her back,
Nit, the Great,
Who gave birth to the beings,
Who created the grains,
Who nourished Her son Shu with Her milk,
She nourishes the Great Words of the Creator inside Aba,
She who rejuvenates Wesir, Lord of Life,

You are the Mistress of Valor, in the Day of Battle,
Who seizes the bow and shoots Her arrows,
Repelling the bands of rebels,
Great is Her Power over the Nine Bows.
And the barbarians fall under Her slaughter,
But She takes Whom She loves to be King,
Eternally, like Heru on the Serekh,

You are the Mistress of Heaven, the Earth, the Underworld
the Waters and Mountains,
Whose prestige is great everywhere,

You are the Mistress of the Palace,
Who protects the Sovereign,
Safeguarding his soldiers
Guardian of the flat countries and mountain countries in their
    totality,
Great *Uraeus* in front of the Gods and Goddesses,
Serpent of Life, Who protects the country;
...by the sovereign, with joy,
As the work of Her person,

One whom Tanen distinguishes to be the Lord of the Myriads,
As well as the golden hawk who is with Her,

You are the one who depends on the enthronement of the King
Because all order comes from Her
One does not enter into the palace without Her knowledge,

You are the Mistress of the Carriers of the Desert,
Lady of the Bracelets,
Mistress of the Eastern Market,
Lady of Punt,
For whom the Palace of the Bee is flooded with perfume,
Whose smell is that of fresh frankincense,
Distills drop on the curls of Her hair,
Whose body is distinguished thanks to the White Crown,
Mistress of *Heh*, Cat Lady,
To whom *Isten* makes the offering,
Mistress *Rochet* and *Tefrer*,
She created all kinds of real, precious stones,
She, the Gentle Patroness of the Stone-*Ankh*,
Lady of Lapis Lazuli, Turquoise and Jasper.[128]

---

[128] Sauneron, Serge, *Esna V: Les fêtes religieuses d'Esna aux derniers siècles du paganisme*, (Cairo: IFAO, 1962; 2004), 110-113. Translated by Chelsea Bolton.

HYMN OF NIT

Adore this Goddess in Great Glory,
Gods and Humans, run,
Bow to the earth before the Mother of God,
For it is Nit that is the surface of the water
and it is Her child that is the Nun,
All that is, is born from Her birth,
And there is nothing that exists apart from what She had made.
She is the Great Ancestor, Who was at the Beginning,
Creator Goddess, Born into the world on Her own,
First Mother, *Uraeus*, Front of the God,
With the hidden name
To be divine at the same time, God and Goddess,
Goddess who is in God,
Eminent Guide to the highest point,
Greater than the Goddesses, because She was the first;
Born before them all
One Who began to be
Before the beings found existence
Because all creatures emerged
After Her birth,
She finally touches the limits of the total universe,
Under Her corporeal aspect as the watery surface,
And under Her true nature of unlimited time,
Because She is Great, very Great of Pace,
Until the Two Limits of Time
The Red Crown and White Crown are Hers,
And the *Uraeus* is marked by Her hieroglyph,
She is the one who produced the sun,

And the light shines in Her every day,

In Her form of Celestial Nut.

Who produced everything in the heart of Her heart,

And having created the earth,

She made the Two Countries that are organized under Her
   direction.

How great is Her power over the Nine Bows!

All foreign countries bow before Her power!

For it is She who confers victory and triumph![129]

[129] Sauneron, Serge, *Esna V: Les fêtes religieuses d'Esna aux derniers siècles du paganisme*, (Cairo: IFAO, 1962; 2004), 281-282. Translated by Chelsea Bolton.

HYMN OF NIT

Guardian Gods take care of Her!
Human Beings beware of Her power!
Men and Women send hymns to Her majesty!
Follow Her, even more than the Gods of the Ennead!
Fear Her, tremble before Her prestige,
For She is an all-powerful deity
Mistress of Fury,
She can manifest against anyone of hostility,
But also knows how to return to calm.
She is the Mistress of the Bow,
Lady of Arrows,
With destructive power,
Who massacres among the rebels,
Great Gold, Powerful of Flame,
Who launches Her fire against any enemy She may have,
And consumes the adversary with the flame,
How good it is to follow Her!
How sweet it is to pray to Her, day and night,
And bow before Her name
Because She is the Lady of Health,
And Life is from Her orders,
She is Great and Powerful,
Regent of Food,
In other words, Tatenen, the Master of Food,
The Great, Renenutet, Wadjet,
Goddess, Mistress of Food,
Mistress of the Anointing Oil as well as the fabrics,
Who returned to Her profession to weave between the five,

...Who inhabits the Sky and the Earth,
Keep in memory Her power
Do not get tired of following Her
Pray,
Exalt Her
Forever![130]

[130] Sauneron, Serge, *Esna V: Les fêtes religieuses d'Esna aux derniers siècles du paganisme*, (Cairo: IFAO, 1962; 2004), 282. Translated by Chelsea Bolton.

HYMN OF NIT

Adoration to You,
As high as the sky,
Veneration,
As wide as the Earth,
Acclaim,
At all times of the duration,
Veneration of Yourself extends
until the limits of the Great Green (the Sea)
Queen at the Beginning of the Year
Princess of the Stars
Who creates Atum in Memphis,
Mistress of the Knife-Making Gods
To whom belong the wandering spirits,
And on the order of whom strike the emissary spirits
Because life and death depend on a single word from Her!
Queen of the Gods of Heaven,
Sovereign of the Gods of the Earth,
and also the Universal Mistress of the Gods of the Underworld,
The First Time of the deities
Originally emerged and began to be,
Before there were those who were to be;
For those who were after, She was first.
One who made the previous gods,
Who creates the high ground,
And gave birth to the sun, who received the name of Ra,
--because His rays reached the earth—
And who made the Gods from His smile when He saw Her;
He began to cry,

When She (Nit) went away from Him,
And the humans were born with the tears from His eye,
Place it on Her head
In Her aspect of the *Akhet*-Cow,
And She swam while wearing it
As Mehet Weret,
She slaughtered the one who rebelled against Her on the water,
She destroyed Apep when Her time came,
And the God remained sitting between Her horns,
While She was in the middle of the water,
Until She reached Sais
On the night of the 13th of Epiphi,
Divine Mother of Ra,
Who creates Atum,
Mehet Weret, Who gave birth to the Words of Creation,
Akhet-Cow, Who created the Eight Gods!
When She reaches Esna
And comes to this place that Her heart cherishes,
In Southern Egypt,
The Eight Gods are in prayer before Her face
And the Great Creator's Words are the safeguard of Her limbs,
Menhuy praises Her,
And Tithoes, the Great Knife-Maker follows Her,
Heru of Shendenu is at Her right side,
The Gods are in joy,
The Goddesses are in joy,
All classes of humans have their heads bowed,
The Sky is celebrating,
The Earth is in joy,
Esna is full of Her blessings,
~because it is Her city of Sais in the country of the South!

She repelled the evil that had sprung up there,
And She shot down the rebels
By the virtue of Her word![131]

---

[131] Sauneron, Serge, *Esna V: Les fêtes religieuses d'Esna aux derniers siècles du paganisme,* (Cairo: IFAO, 1962; 2004), 288-289. Translated by Chelsea Bolton.

HYMN OF NIT

Sopdet, Queen of the Stars
Seshat, the Great, Mistress of Writing,
........under Her fear,
The earth is under Her prestige,
Flat countries and mountains tremble for fear of Her!
She who resides on the throne in the width of the Sky ,
Holy and secret in the Mysterious Portico,
Eternal
Whose image resides on the side of Her son Wesir,
Eternal, eternal,
Living, Living
Menhyt, when She flows with the inundation,
Nebetuu, also, who gives birth to everything,
Creates plants
Brings cereals
In order to give birth to any seed for Her creatures
Because She ensures the food of Gods and Humans,

She opens Her granary
At the Feast of the Great Flame (Rekh Wer)
At the 8th of the month of Mechir,
To give the food offerings to the Gods,

However all humans live on the supplement of Her loaves,
She opens Her palace
At the Feast of Khoiak,
At the 27th of the month of Khoiak,
For the offering of incense

and all fragrant products,
in order to anoint the god:
iber, hekenu
tichepes, medj,
tep and all the sweet and fragrant products.

She opens Her palace
At the Festival of the Valley,
At the 26th of the month of Payni,
In order to dress the gods,
To put on the God-Father of such fabric.
....
And any fabric related to the engagement of divine worship
Her heart is happy in the Palace of the Father
And the Palace of the Mother is flooded with Her blessings,
Pi-Neter is sanctified to possess Her chapel.[132]

---

[132] Sauneron, Serge, *Esna V: Les fêtes religieuses d'Esna aux derniers siècles du paganisme*, (Cairo: IFAO, 1962; 2004), 289-291. Translated by Chelsea Bolton.

HYMN OF NIT

Mistress of the Land of God
Sovereign of Punt
Lady of any country,
Mut in *Isheru*,
Nekhbet in El-Kab,
Beloved of Ptah in Ankh-Tawy,
Nubet in Ouah-to,
Ureret in Sais,
Hethert in every nome,
Mistress of Fury
Who conquers as Sekhmet
Whose Majesty is inducted like Bast,
Who put Heru in the world as the King of the Gods,
And conquers for Him the Two Halves of Egypt, triumphantly
Great Name at the Head of the Gods,
Even more glorious than the Ennead,
Effective Goddess, from whom everything depends,
The Goddess has an effective mouth,
To the Crowns of Success
.................to Her only,
The Sovereign is crowned at Her wish,
Life and death are in Her fist.
Destiny and fortune are at the orders of Herself,
Because no act is accomplished without Her,
Great of the Greats,
As no one is greater than She,
As She has no likeness in Upper and Lower Egypt,
There is no creature, in Heaven or on Earth

Who did not come after Her,
She did the moment
She created the hours,
She created the years,
She created the months,
She gave birth to the season of flood,
To the winter, to the summer,
She created the sand,
She created the Earth,
And Sais was born...[133]

[133] Sauneron, Serge, *Esna V: Les fêtes religieuses d'Esna aux derniers siècles du paganisme*, (Cairo: IFAO, 1962; 2004), 291-292. Translated by Chelsea Bolton.

HYMN OF NIT

Sais, it is the district that occurred at the Beginning,
As well as Esna in Upper Egypt
It is called Khent-to, the tip of the country,
She turned Her face toward Pi-Neter, north of Esna,
It is a holy place without its equal,
To ensure the funeral provisions of Wesir, Lord of Aba,
And the dead who are in His wake,
People stand and lie down in His honor,
And vice-versa;
Anguish is addressed to Him in the Morning Prayers
The sacred balanite blossoms with life, without ceasing
Atum and His children are in joy
The Guard of the 4th Day is in gladness for You,
The Guard of the 6th Day is in jubilation for Your Majesty
Djehuty rejoices and likes to contemplate You
The inhabitants of the Great Place
Wesir, the Protector,
Yinepu, the Imy-Pe,
Heret, Daughter of Ra,
...................and Nebetuu,
Play the tambourine in Your name.

Pi-Khnum of the Country is in Awe
And Cries of Joy
For the opponent is far away from the Palace of the Ba,
And the rebel is condemned to the pyre
Apep is fallen, shredded;
The Crew of Ra is in joy

The inhabitants of Esna are jubilant
The Palace of the Two Birds is in joy
May Your heart be happy
Birth Mother, Creator of Eternity
Behind whom passes eternity and durability
And Who sees before Her millions of years
Until the limits of time.[134]

---

[134] Sauneron, Serge, *Esna V: Les fêtes religieuses d'Esna aux derniers siècles du paganisme*, (Cairo: IFAO, 1962; 2004), 292. Translated by Chelsea Bolton.

HYMN OF NIT

The sky is in Festival
The earth is in joy,
The temples are moved with delight,
The gods cheer
The goddesses show their joy,
The people venerate Her face,
Nit, the Great, the Powerful One,
Who made the beings,
Who spread joy in Her city,
Who makes Her morning appearance in Her palace,
Accompanied by all life, all dominion, all power,
Nut, the Great repels the storm clouds,
Hunting the rain in front of Her
So that the Sky shines
And the Earth is bright
For Nut, the Great stands
To form the vault.

We order the festival a second time,
The Day of the Festival to Lift Up the Sky
Because Tatenen appears a second time
Eternity is the name given to Her majesty,
She is actually Tatenen,
Two-thirds of Her are male,
One-third is female,
She creates the rays of light,
Chasing the darkness
Revealing the solar disk with Her luminous brilliance,

And concealing it in Her pupil
When She rises (at sunrise)
She gives birth to Her light,
So that everyone can distinguish oneself from their companion,
Appearing in the form of the moon,
She is still chasing darkness
For it is Nut in which the God of the Horizon rises and sets,
The Goddess who has no physical limits
And of which we cannot know the temporal limits,
Bright as the sun,
Rising as the moon,
She illuminates the shores with Her splendor,
She made what is,
She created the beings,
Generating all things endowed with life,
Heaven is the name given to Her majesty,
She gave the beginning to the Earth according to Her plans,
And She made everything as the creation of Her heart,
When She crosses the sky following Her heart,
Her son Ra is joyous before Her,
The two arms are raised in adoration
Before the Mistress of the Gods.

Forming hymns of gratitude to Her powerful mother,
At the moment, when She is giving birth to one child in the
    morning,
Ra Himself addresses the Morning Song to Himself,
Young man having passed a certain age,
It is now Ra Heru Akhety, who acclaims His splendor,
Mankind having attained the strength of age,
Finally, Atum kissed the ground before Her face,
Gods and Goddesses are in adoration,
And the First Primordial Ones bow before Her power,

The entire Great Ennead and the Small Ennead bow their heads,
The Great Horizon,
There is no more darkness in the clouds
For the Mistress of Fear has illuminated the earth,
The gods of the south bow,
The gods of the north bow their heads,
Those of the west welcome Her
And the east is in adoration!

The inhabitants in the horizon adore Her splendor,
The souls of the East cheer and shout: Bow down!
And the Great Gods united in a single group,
Behold their mother,
At the same time, the God and Goddess
And each God said to their companion:

Let us address praises to the Queen of the Gods,
Exalt the Great One of Prestige.
Let us show our joy to the Lady of Love,
Let us reconcile the favor of the All Powerful One in Her cabin,
Let us shout in honor of the Cow of Heaven,
Satisfied by our praise,
The heart of the Lady of Heaven and Earth,
Let us fulfill the desires of the Divine Mother of Ra,
Let us prostrate in honor of the Lady of the South and North,
Sanctify the ground to the worthy and powerful Goddess,
When She comes to the Horizon of the Sky,
One whose perfume wafts from Punt
Whose smell is that of dried frankincense,
Solar Goddess, Who is bright in Her appearance,
Whose adornment is greater than the adornment of the South and
    North,
Like the sky when cleansed by a heavy rain.

One who has no equal
There is no one like Her,
Who illuminates the sky with the light of Her eyes,
Who illuminates the desert with Her eyes,
Her boat is beautiful gold, sparkling with decoration,
And of all kinds of precious gemstones,
Each god stands at their office,
The crew of Her boat is in joy,
Her holy cabin is in joy,
While we hail Her owner
The gods that are there are in joy,
The musician goddesses of the South and North,
Raise their arms in adoration,
The Souls of Pe and Nekhen gesture with their arms
Before Her power
And Her boat progresses
Without Her navigation being interrupted by anything
In the Palace of Nit,
And all of Egypt is in festival,
For the divine being, at the same time God and Goddess,
Shines above their heads,
And every eye gives thanks for Her rays,
Every country is illuminated by Her bright radiance,
Her cabin also spreads the light,
For those who are in the Underworld,
And the inhabitants of the Land of the Dead rejoice at Her sight.[135]

[135] Sauneron, Serge, *Esna V: Les fêtes religieuses d'Esna aux derniers siècles du paganisme*, (Cairo: IFAO, 1962; 2004), 151-154. Translated by Chelsea Bolton. Thank you to Tamara L. Siuda for her help with this translation.

HYMN OF NIT

The whole country is illuminated with Your blessings,
As Your face is beautiful,
when You draw the flood from its cave,
The country is flooded with Your kindness,
and Egypt shines with Your blessings!

As Your face is beautiful,
When You are the Mistress of the Countryside,
Blowing through the wind to grow plants
and create food for everyone.

As Your face is beautiful,
in the season of the flood,
when you grow the plants,
fatten the seeds,
and give birth to the Tree of Life for the Living!

How beautiful is Your face,
In the winter season,
When the countryside blossoms from the vegetation,
You speak about everything that comes out of it!

As Your face is beautiful,
In the summer season,
When You fill the palace, roof and granary
And assure the divine offerings to the Gods and Goddesses.[136]

---

[136] Sauneron, Serge, *Esna V: Les fêtes religieuses d'Esna aux derniers siècles du paganisme*, (Cairo: IFAO, 1962; 2004), 161. Translated by Chelsea Bolton.

HYMN OF NIT

Father of Fathers, Mother of Mothers,
The divine being who began to be in the Beginning,
Was in the Primordial Waters,
Who appeared by Herself
When the earth was still in darkness,
When no earth had yet appeared,
When no plant grew...

She gave Herself the appearance of the Cow,
That no divine being,
Or the following could yet know,
Then She turned into a *lates*-fish and made Her way...

She says then:
The place where I am becoming for Me
This platform of land,
Was placed on the waters of the Primordial Waters,
So that I can build upon it.

This place where Nit was
Became a platform within the Primordial Waters,
As She said.
And it was the Land of Water (Esna)
Where Nit was becoming
She took flight over this emergence,
Which was Pi-Neter,
Which was also Buto.

She says:
I feel good about this emergence,
This is how Dep came to be,
This is how the Land of Goodness came to be,
Which became the name of Sais.

However all that Her heart conceived was realized at once,
So She conceived the wellbeing of this emergence,
And Egypt was, in joy.

She created the thirty gods,
By pronouncing their names, one by one,
And then joy seized Her after She had seen Them.

Hail to You, Mistress of the Divine Entrances,
Our Mother, who gave us existence!
You made our names, while we were not yet aware.
You have separated for us,
The White Dawn from the Night,
You have made for us
A ground on which we can stand,
You have separated for us,
The night from the day,
What effectiveness, what effectiveness,
In everything that comes out of Your heart,
You, the only one coming into existence at the Beginning,
The eternal duration of time passes before Your face.

This God was born of the execrations of the body of Nit,
She had placed the body in this egg,
When it burst in the Primordial Waters,
It was the first of the water rising, at a single point;
The seed fell on the egg,

when it broke the shell that was around the holy God:
it was Ra,
who was hidden in the Primordial Waters
in His name of Amun, the Ancient One,
who formed the Gods and Goddesses with His rays
in His name of Khnum.

His mother, the Cow Goddess,
Called out in a loud voice:
Come, come, you whom I have created!
Come, come, you whom I gave birth to!
Come, come, you whom I've brought to life!
I am your mother, the *Akhet*-Cow!

This god came, smiling, with open arms,
Towards this Goddess,
He embraced Her,
For that is what a son does when he sees his mother.

And this day became the beautiful day of the Beginning of the Year,
Then he wept in the Primordial Waters,
When he no longer saw his mother, the *Akhet*-Cow,
And humans were born from the tears from His eye,
And he salivated when he saw her again,
And the gods were born with the saliva from his lips.

The Primordial Gods rest in their naos;
They had been expressed as this Goddess had conceived them in
    Her mind.
They protect Ra inside the cabin,
And they hail this God, saying:
Welcome, Welcome to You,
Offspring of Nit,

Work of Her hands,
Creation of Her heart,
You are the King of this Land
Forever
As Your mother had foretold.

However the Primordial Gods were repulsed by a spitting from
    Nit's mouth
Which She had produced in the Primordial Waters
It turned into a snake of elbows
It was named Apep,
His heart conceived the revolt against Ra
With his associates coming from His eye.

Now seven words were spoken successively from Her mouth:
They became the Seven Divine Beings,
For what She had proclaimed
She gave the name to the Words
She gave the name to the Word of God
She also gave the name to Sais.
Thus were born the Seven Words
Which became the Gods of Mehet Weret
Whom ensured the protection of Mehet Weret
Wherever She went.
Then She changed into the *Akhet*-Cow
She placed Ra between Her horns
And She swam while carrying Him.
And the Gods said: Here is the Great Swimmer with Her son.
This was the origin of the name Mehet Weret.

When She reached Sais
On the evening of the 13th of Epiphi,
It was a Beautiful and Great Festival

In Heaven, on Earth and in every country.
She then took the form of the Goddess Ureret,
She seized Her bow in Her hand,
Her arrow in Her fist,
And She settled at the Palace of Nit,
With Her son Ra.

Ra, then said to the Gods with Him:
Welcome, Nit, on this day!
Come and enjoy Yourself on this beautiful day!
For She has brought Me here, safe and sound.
Ignite torches before Her!
Celebrate in Her presence until dawn![137]

---

[137] Sauneron, Serge, *Esna V: Les fêtes religieuses d'Esna aux derniers siècles du paganisme*, (Cairo: IFAO, 1962; 2004), 253-270.

HYMN OF NIT

Given the Third of the Summer,
To enter into the Palace of Nit,
To make a solemn oblation,
Consisting of all good things,
To proclaim the processional ritual of this Goddess,
That the Lector Priest announces Her coming,
Until the third hour of the day.

She who appears in Procession,
The Mother of Mothers, Nit,
The Great, Mother of God,
Mistress of Esna,
As well as Her divine college,
To carry a bow in front of Her,
By the very great prince,
As well as the signs, to unite with the disc,
To halt upon the return to the Great Hall,
While Her divine college halts also,
To Her right and to Her left,
Perfom all the Rites of Her Epiphany.
An offering is made,
Solemn and divine,
Consisting of:
Bread, white bread,
Cakes, beer,
Wine, all good things,
Chedeh, Honey,
Milk, Fruits,

Vegetables,

Flowers,

Incense on the flame,

Oxen, Poultry,

Silver, Gold,

Perfume, Frankincense,

In the whole temple,

Both inside and out.

Perform the food service,

As to make the divine offering every day,

By the Great Purifier,

Who is in service of this day.

To reveal the face of the God of the City,

To reveal the face of the Goddess Nit,

Read the book of hymns relating to this day,

Adore both crowns,

To purify the divine college with water,

Sanctify this temple in its entirety,

However, the Head Lector-Priest,

A golden menat and faience is around his/her neck,

Decorated with the face of a ram, shoulders covered with hackles,

An ostrich feather on Her head, stands before this Goddess,

Face turned to the North,

Perfom the ritual appropriate to this day,

Before this Goddess.[138]

---

[138] Sauneron, Serge, *Esna V: Les fêtes religieuses d'Esna aux derniers siècles du paganisme*, (Cairo: IFAO, 1962; 2004), 278. Translated by Chelsea Bolton. Pterophore is the Greek name for Lector Priest.

HYMN OF NIT

Return to Her temple, in peace,
To be said by the Priests:
Ohe! Ohe!
Here She is!
Come in Joy!
Nit, the Great Cow, come in peace!
Ohe, Ohe
For Her arrival
Nit, the Great, Mother of God,
Mistress of Esna,
Menhyt-Nebetuu, Mistress of Khent-to,
The appearance of this Goddess and Her divine college!
At Her headquarters,
Light many torches inside the temple,
That men and women are celebrating,
That this whole city shouts in joy,
And that no one, until dawn, will sleep,
That it will be a feast![139]

---

[139] Sauneron, Serge, *Esna V: Les fêtes religieuses d'Esna aux derniers siècles du paganisme*, (Cairo: IFAO, 1962; 2004), 302. Translated by Chelsea Bolton.

HYMN FROM CANOPIC BOX OF NS-'3-RWD (BM EA 8539)

Hail to you, Nit, the Great
Mother of God, Hidden of Form within Sais,
the Braided One, Enduring of Love,
Beloved of Her heir,
the Good Nurse of the Noble Child,
Who nurses him everyday
Who conducts the clothing of the mummy
as She protects the body of the god,
She who makes his protection daily,
Who causes that he rests in the sarcophagus
Who binds his name as the strong bull.[140]

---

[140] Ouda, Ahmed M. Mekawy. "The Canopic Box of NS-'3-RWD (BM EA 8539)." *The Journal of Egyptian Archaeology 98, no. 1* (2012): 132 and 134. I changed Neith to her ancient Egyptian name Nit.

HYMNS OF NUT

(Nuit)

HYMN OF NUT

Nut, the Great,
Who Gave Birth to the Gods and Goddesses,
Princess, Mistress of the Heavenly,
Nurse of Great Power,
Strong One, Who is Like No Other,
Nut, the Great, Who Gave Birth to the Gods.[141]

---

[141] Kockelmann, Holger and Erich Winter, *Philae III: Die Zweite Ostkolonnade des Tempels der Isis in Philae. (CO II und CO II K)*, (Verlag der Osterreichischen Akademie der Wissenschaften/Austrian Academy of Sciences, 2016), 24-25. Translated by Chelsea Bolton.

Hymn of Nut

Nut, the Great,
Who gives birth to the Gods
Mistress of the Sky,
Sister of Goddesses.[142]

---

[142] Kockelmann, Holger and Erich Winter, *Philae III: Die Zweite Ostkolonnade des Tempels der Isis in Philae. (CO II und CO II K)*, (Verlag der Osterreichischen Akademie der Wissenschaften/Austrian Academy of Sciences, 2016), 265-266. Translated by Chelsea Bolton.

HYMN OF NUT

O, Great One, Sky
You made power and strength,
and filled every place with Your beauty,
All lands belong to You.
You hold Geb and all creation in Your embrace.[143]

---

[143] Siuda, Tamara L., *The Ancient Egyptian Prayerbook*, (Illinois: Stargazer Design, 2009), 73-74.

HYMNS OF SEKHMET

HYMN OF SEKHMET

Sekhmet, the Great
Who resides in Senmet,
Mistress of the *Per Wer*,
Regent of the *Per Neser*,
She who repels the enemies of Her Father Ra
In the Castle of Flame.[144]

---

[144] Inconnu-Bocquillon, Danielle, *Le mythe de la déesse lointaine à Philae, BdE 132*, (Le Caire/Cairo: IFAO, 2001), 25.

HYMN OF SEKHMET

Sekhmet, the Great,
Lady of Flame in Senmet,
Wepeset, the Flame
Regent of the Abaton,
Venerable, Coiled One on the Head of the One of the Horizon,
One who consumes Apep by the burning breath of Her mouth,
Mistress of Carnage, among the enemies of Her Father Ra,
One who throws their bones into the Abaton.[145]

---

[145] Inconnu-Bocquillon, Danielle, *Le mythe de la déesse lointaine à Philae, BdE 132*, (Le Caire/Cairo: IFAO, 2001), 36.

HYMN OF SEKHMET

Sekhmet, the Great,
Lady of Flame in Senmet,
Wepeset, Lady of Flame,
Regent of the Castle of Flame,
Who reduces to ashes the bad-of-character with Her flame,
Great Flame,
Who consumes the aggressors,
Flame,
Who springs up against them quickly,
As long as Sekhmet will be powerful in Senmet in Her Forms,
As the Eye of Heru lives,
The one flame surrounds it.
To consume the enemy with the burning breath of Her mouth,
She is *Qerhet* (Most Noble Goddess)
August, Standing on Her tail
To throw the burning breath
Against the enemies of Her Father.[146]

---

[146] Inconnu-Bocquillon, Danielle, *Le mythe de la déesse lointaine à Philae, BdE 132*, (Le Caire/Cairo: IFAO, 2001), 42. Thank you to Tamara L. Siuda for her help with this translation. Qerhet means "Most Noble Goddess" and can also be a Cobra form as an Eye of Ra.

HYMN OF SEKHMET

Sekhmet, the Great,
Lady of Flame in Senmet,
Living Flame, Who Devours what exists,
Djehuty is in Her company to appease Her.[147]

---

[147] Inconnu-Bocquillon, Danielle, *Le mythe de la déesse lointaine à Philae, BdE 132*, (Le Caire/Cairo: IFAO, 2001), 56.

HYMN OF SEKHMET

Sekhmet,
Lady of Flame in Senmet,
August and Perfect,
in the House of Ptah.[148]

---

[148] Inconnu-Bocquillon, Danielle, *Le mythe de la déesse lointaine à Philae, BdE 132*, (Le Caire/Cairo: IFAO, 2001), 61.

HYMN OF SEKHMET

Sekhmet, the Great
Lady of the Fiery Flame in Senmet,
Eye of Ra,
Only One in the Castle of the *Ka* of Ptah,
Beloved of Ptah, in Memphis.[149]

---

[149] Inconnu-Bocquillon, Danielle, *Le mythe de la déesse lointaine à Philae, BdE 132*, (Le Caire/Cairo: IFAO, 2001), 77.

HYMN OF SEKHMET

Sekhmet, the Great,
Lady of Flame in Senmet,
Eye of Ra, Lady of Flame,
At the Head of the Castle of Flame,
Mistress of Terror, Regent of the Gods,
Who reduces the mountain to ashes with Her flame,
As long as Sekhmet will be in the Abaton as the Eye of Ra,
Venerable, Regent of the Gods,
To transmit light
To chase away darkness,
To illuminate the Earth with Her Two Luminous Eyes,
She will be the Mistress of Heaven,
Uraeus of Her Father,
Perfect Luminous Eye,
Regent of the Goddesses.[150]

---

[150] Inconnu-Bocquillon, Danielle, *Le mythe de la déesse lointaine à Philae, BdE 132*, (Le Caire/Cairo: IFAO, 2001), 96.

HYMN OF SEKHMET

Sekhmet, the Great,
Tefnut in Senmet,
Who unites with Her brother,
Who Causes *Bau* to Flourish (Shu),
In the Abaton.[151]

---

[151] Inconnu-Bocquillon, Danielle, *Le mythe de la déesse lointaine à Philae, BdE 132*, (Le Caire/Cairo: IFAO, 2001), 119. Thank you to Tamara L. Siuda for her help with this translation.

HYMN TO SEKHMET

Sekhmet, Who burns the adversaries
Powerful One, Great in Carnage
Those opponents
Iabt, Her Father's opponents
Flame Goddess, who burns the enemies
Sekhmet, the Great, Beloved of Ptah.[152]

---

[152] Kockelmann, Holger and Erich Winter, *Philae III: Die Zweite Ostkolonnade des Tempels der Isis in Philae. (CO II und CO II K)*, (Verlag der Osterreichischen Akademie der Wissenschaften/Austrian Academy of Sciences, 2016), 36-37. Thank you to Inanna Gruner for her help with this translation.

HYMN TO SEKHMET

Sekhmet, the Great
Lady of the Flame in Senmet.[153]

---

[153] Kockelmann, Holger and Erich Winter, *Philae III: Die Zweite Ostkolonnade des Tempels der Isis in Philae. (CO II und CO II K)*, (Verlag der Osterreichischen Akademie der Wissenschaften/Austrian Academy of Sciences, 2016), 182.

JUBILATION TO SEKHMET

I ask that You hear, Golden One!
I beg Your heart turn to me!
Hail, Lady of Plague,
Sekhmet, the Great, Lady of Ladies!
Praised by Her father,
Eldest of Her creator,
At the prow of Ra's boat
Roaming loose in its cabin!
Your arms make light,
Your rays brighten the Lands.
The Two Lands are under Your rule
And the *Remetj* are Your people![154]

---

[154] Siuda, Tamara L., The *Ancient Egyptian Prayerbook*, (Stargazer Design, 2009), 75. Theban Tomb 60 (TT60), Middle Kingdom

PRAYER TO SEKHMET

Hail Sekhmet among the Great,
Lady of Heaven, Mistress of the Two Lands,
Who does what She wishes
Among the gods in their shrines.
All men are in awe of You,
Lady of Life within Wadjet.[155]

---

[155] Siuda, Tamara L., The *Ancient Egyptian Prayerbook*, (Stargazer Design, 2009), 75. CT 651.

HYMN TO SEKHMET

Hail to thee, Lady of Fragrance,
Great Sekhmet, Sovereign Lady,
Worshiped One,
Serpent who is upon her father...
Your rays illumine the Two Lands
The Two Regions are beneath Your sway.[156]

---

[156] Lesko, Barbara, *The Great Goddesses of Egypt*, (Oklahoma: University of Oklahoma Press, 1999), 103. This is a chorus from a hymn to Hethert.

Brooklyn Museum Papyrus 47.218.50

Sekhmet, Eye of Ra
Sekhmet, Beloved of Ptah
Sekhmet, Devouring Flame
Sekhmet, Lady of *Isheru*.[157]

---

[157] Goyon, J.-Cl, *Confirmation du pouvoir royal au Nouvel An: Brooklyn Museum Papyrus 47.218.50, BdE 52*, (Cairo: IFAO, 1972), 65. Translated by Chelsea Bolton.

HYMNS OF SERQET

(Serket; Selket; Selkis)

Hymn from Canopic Box of NS-'3-RWD (BM EA 8539)

Serqet, God's Wife, Beloved of her husband,
the noble and the powerful one,
Who came forth from the primeval water,
the noble serpent, Great of Awe,
Who heals every snakebite,
Who seized the Two Lands in glory,
Lady of Speech, Great of Magic,
Who causes people and gods to live,
Who causes to breathe after misery,
Who gives the breath in...?[158]

---

[158] Ouda, Ahmed M. Mekawy. "The Canopic Box of NS-'3-RWD (BM EA 8539)." *The Journal of Egyptian Archaeology 98, no. 1* (2012): 132 and 134. I changed Serket to Serqet.

HYMNS OF SESHAT

(Sefkhet-Awby)

HYMN TO SESHAT

Hail to You,
Noble Lady, Female Ruler,
Mistress of Goddesses,
Seshat, the Great,
Lady of Writing.[159]

---

[159] Adapted from a translation by Barbara A. Richter in Richter, Barbara A., *The Theology of Hathor of Dendera: Aural and Visual Scribal Techniques in the Per-Wer Sanctuary*, (Lockwood Press, 2016), 301. Translated by Barbara A. Richter. Used with permission.

Hymn of Seshat

Seshat, the Primordial One
Who initiated writing.[160]

---

[160] Adapted from a translation by Barbara A. Richter in Richter, Barbara A., *The Theology of Hathor of Dendera: Aural and Visual Scribal Techniques in the Per-Wer Sanctuary*, (Lockwood Press, 2016), 503. Translated by Barbara A. Richter. Used with permission.

Hymn of Seshat

The Female King of Upper and Lower Egypt,
Seshat, the Primordial One,
Who created writing,
Lady of Writing,
Female Ruler of Papyrus Books,
Noble and Powerful Lady,
Without another except for Her,
The *Atenet* who shines in the sky.
What goes forth from Her mouth comes into being at once.
Hethert, the Great, Lady of Iunet.[161]

---

[161] Adapted from a translation by Barbara A. Richter in Richter, Barbara A., *The Theology of Hathor of Dendera: Aural and Visual Scribal Techniques in the Per-Wer Sanctuary*, (Lockwood Press, 2016), 341. Translated by Barbara A. Richter. Used with permission.

HYMN OF SESHAT

The Female King of Upper and Lower Egypt,
Seshat, the Primordial One,
Who invented writing,
Lady of Writing, Female Ruler of Scrolls,
Noble and Powerful Lady,
Without another except for Her,
The *Atenet*, who shines in the sky,
What goes forth from Her mouth comes into being at once.
Hethert, the Great, Lady of Iunet.[162]

---

[162] Adapted from a translation by Barbara A. Richter in Richter, Barbara A., *The Theology of Hathor of Dendera: Aural and Visual Scribal Techniques in the Per-Wer Sanctuary*, (Lockwood Press, 2016), 380. Translated by Barbara A. Richter. Used with permission.

HYMN OF SESHAT

Seshat, the Female Creator
Who created writing,
Lady of Writing,
Female Ruler of Scrolls.[163]

---

[163] Adapted from a translation by Barbara A. Richter in Richter, Barbara A., *The Theology of Hathor of Dendera: Aural and Visual Scribal Techniques in the Per-Wer Sanctuary*, (Lockwood Press, 2016), 261. Translated by Barbara A. Richter. Used with permission.

Excerpt Hymn of Seshat

Seshat, the Great,
Princess of the Library
Great of Magic,
Princess of All the Gods.[164]

---

[164] Kockelmann, Holger and Erich Winter, *Philae III: Die Zweite Ostkolonnade des Tempels der Isis in Philae. (CO II und CO II K)*, (Verlag der Osterreichischen Akademie der Wissenschaften/Austrian Academy of Sciences, 2016), 143. Translated by Chelsea Bolton. I changed Isis to her ancient Egyptian name Aset.

HYMN OF SESHAT

Seshat, the Great,
Princess of the Library,
Lady of Writing,
One who provides the texts,
Guarded in Her vicinity.[165]

---

[165] Kockelmann, Holger and Erich Winter, *Philae III: Die Zweite Ostkolonnade des Tempels der Isis in Philae. (CO II und CO II K)*, (Verlag der Osterreichischen Akademie der Wissenschaften/Austrian Academy of Sciences, 2016), 141. Translated by Chelsea Bolton.

HYMNS OF TEFNUT

(Tefenet)

HYMN OF TEFNUT

Tefnut, Daughter of Ra
Who resides in Senmet,
Lady of the Flame in the Castle of Flame,
Queen of Upper and Lower Egypt,
Female Ra, Regent of the Two Lands
Great Sovereign in the Chapel,
August and Powerful, Who springs from Kenset,
Who attends Senmet in the form of the Venerable Wepeset.[166]

---

[166] Inconnu-Bocquillon, Danielle, *Le mythe de la déesse lointaine à Philae*, *BdE 132*, (Le Caire/Cairo: IFAO, 2001), 22.

HYMN OF TEFNUT

Tefnut, Daughter of Ra,
Uraeus on His forehead,
Eye of Ra, Lady of Senmet,
The beauty on the Head of Her Father,
With the Beautiful Face, Sweet of Love
Mother, Who Gives Birth to the Gods.[167]

---

[167] Inconnu-Bocquillon, Danielle, *Le mythe de la déesse lointaine à Philae, BdE 132*, (Le Caire/Cairo: IFAO, 2001), 23.

HYMN OF TEFNUT

Tefnut, Daughter of Ra,
Wepeset,
Lady of Flame in the Castle of Flame,
One who consumes Apep with the burning breath of Her mouth,
Venerable Wife of Her brother Shu,
Who does not stray from Him to any other place.[168]

---

[168] Inconnu-Bocquillon, Danielle, *Le mythe de la déesse lointaine à Philae, BdE 132*, (Le Caire/Cairo: IFAO, 2001), 39.

HYMN OF TEFNUT

Tefnut, Daughter of Ra,
Mistress of the Human Race,
Regent,
Venerable,
Coiled One on the Head of Her Father,
One Who consumes the enemies
With the burning breath of Her mouth.[169]

---

[169] Inconnu-Bocquillon, Danielle, *Le mythe de la déesse lointaine à Philae, BdE 132*, (Le Caire/Cairo: IFAO, 2001), 43.

HYMN OF TEFNUT

Tefnut, Daughter of Ra,
Who resides in the Abaton,
August and Perfect,
Regent of Philae,
One who comes from Kenset to Senmet,
And takes Her seat.[170]

---

[170] Inconnu-Bocquillon, Danielle, *Le mythe de la déesse lointaine à Philae*, *BdE 132*, (Le Caire/Cairo: IFAO, 2001), 45.

HYMN OF TEFNUT

Tefnut, Daughter of Ra,
Who resides in Senmet,
Great of Carnage on the Place of Execution,
Who flies against the enemies of Her son
One who dismembers Her enemies,
Queen of Upper and Lower Egypt,
Female *Ba* greater than the Gods,
Higher than the Goddesses,
Mistress of Battle,
Lioness,
Mistress of Skinning
Superior of the Place of Execution in Eastern Behdet,
One who devours relative to Her height.[171]

---

[171] Inconnu-Bocquillon, Danielle, *Le mythe de la déesse lointaine à Philae, BdE 132*, (Le Caire/Cairo: IFAO, 2001), 50.

HYMN OF TEFNUT

Tefnut, Daughter of Ra
Lady of Senmet,
Great Flame in the Castle of Flame,
Eye of Ra, Mistress of Heaven,
Regent of All the Gods.[172]

---

[172] Inconnu-Bocquillon, Danielle, *Le mythe de la déesse lointaine à Philae*, BdE 132, (Le Caire/Cairo: IFAO, 2001), 51.

HYMN OF TEFNUT

Tefnut, Daughter of Ra
Who resides in the Abaton,
One who consumes Apep,
the enemy of Her Father Ra,
Whose heart rejoices when He sees Her.
Tefnut, Daughter of Ra,
Who resides in the Abaton,
Wepeset,
Lady of Flame in the Castle of Flame,
Tefnut, Daughter of Ra,
Lady of the Abaton,
Great Flame surrounding Him,
One who is stable in Elephantine
One who appears in Senmet.[173]

---

[173] Inconnu-Bocquillon, Danielle, *Le mythe de la déesse lointaine à Philae*, BdE 132, (Le Caire/Cairo: IFAO, 2001), 57.

HYMN OF TEFNUT

Tefnut, Daughter of Ra
Who resides in the Abaton,
August and Powerful,
Regent of Philae,
One from Kenset,
In the company of Her brother.[174]

---

[174] Inconnu-Bocquillon, Danielle, *Le mythe de la déesse lointaine à Philae, BdE 132*, (Le Caire/Cairo: IFAO, 2001), 61.

HYMN OF TEFNUT

Tefnut, Daughter of Ra,
Lady of the Abaton,
Great Flame surrounding Him,
Flame Who shoots out,
Stable in Elephantine,
Appearing in Senmet,
Queen of Upper and Lower Egypt
Daughter of Ra, whom Her heart loves,
One from Ta-Sety,
This is the seat where Wepeset stands
While She is angry,
When She comes from Bugem.[175]

---

[175] Inconnu-Bocquillon, Danielle, *Le mythe de la déesse lointaine à Philae, BdE 132*, (Le Caire/Cairo: IFAO, 2001), 78.

HYMN OF TEFNUT

Tefnut, *Uraeus*
Daughter of Ra,
At the Head of the House of Flame,
Lady of Flame
Who ignites the Two Hills
With the burning breath from Her mouth.[176]

---

[176] Inconnu-Bocquillon, Danielle, *Le mythe de la déesse lointaine à Philae*, BdE 132, (Le Caire/Cairo: IFAO, 2001), 80.

HYMN OF TEFNUT

Tefnut, Daughter of Ra in Senmet,
Venerable,
Uraeus of Heruakhety,
Flame,
Powerful, Regent of the Spirits and Emissaries
One who consumes the enemies with the burning breath of Her
  mouth,
At this place,
Her majesty returns to the land of the Pure Place,
One who burns Apep with Her flame,
As long as Sekhmet is Powerful in Senmet
Burning enemies with Her burning breath
She will burst like flame to the sky,
Then Her name will be Sopdet.[177]

---

[177] Inconnu-Bocquillon, Danielle, *Le mythe de la déesse lointaine à Philae, BdE 132*, (Le Caire/Cairo: IFAO, 2001), 83.

HYMN OF TEFNUT

Tefnut, Daughter of Ra,
Who resides in the Abaton,
Eye of Ra, Mistress of Heaven,
Who is at the Head of Philae,
August and Powerful,
Regent of All the Gods,
Flame, Who burns Her enemies,
Who is appeased by the glorification of the Two Sistra,
As long as the August and Venerable One
Is the One Who appears in Philae,
As Mistress of the Red Cloth, Who Loves Brightness
To receive the *Seshesh*-Sistrum and the *Sekhem*-Sistrum,
In gold, so that Her heart is appeased by their sight,
She is the Lady of Flame,
Who burns Her Father's enemies,
Tefnut, Daughter of Ra,
Who resides in the Abaton.[178]

---

[178] Inconnu-Bocquillon, Danielle, *Le mythe de la déesse lointaine à Philae*, BdE 132, (Le Caire/Cairo: IFAO, 2001), 86.

HYMN OF TEFNUT

Queen of Upper and Lower Egypt
August and Powerful,
Eye of Ra,
Venerable,
Coiled One on the Head of Her Father,
One who shoots Apep with Her burning breath,
in the morning boat,
Tefnut, Daughter of Ra,
Who resides in the Abaton.[179]

---

[179] Inconnu-Bocquillon, Danielle, *Le mythe de la déesse lointaine à Philae, BdE 132*, (Le Caire/Cairo: IFAO, 2001), 87.

HYMN OF TEFNUT

Tefnut, Daughter of Ra,
Who resides in the Abaton,
Regent and Lady of Philae,
Uraeus,
Her Father rejoices to see Her,
Tefnut, Daughter of Ra,
Who resides in the Abaton,
Eye of Ra, Mistress of Heaven,
Who is at the Head of Philae,
August and Venerable,
Regent of All the Gods,
Flame,
Who burns Her enemies,
One who is appeased by the Two Lights
As long as the August and Venerable is the Perfect One,
Daughter of Ra, Who Loves Her,
To receive the *wensheb* from the arms of Ra's son,
To rejoice in Her heart to see Her,
She is the Eye of Ra,
Who illuminates the Two Lands,
Tefnut,
One who resides in the Castle of the Front.[180]

---

[180] Inconnu-Bocquillon, Danielle, *Le mythe de la déesse lointaine à Philae*, BdE 132, (Le Caire/Cairo: IFAO, 2001), 88.

HYMN OF TEFNUT

Tefnut, Daughter of Ra,
Who resides in the Abaton,
Regent of the Goddesses,
Queen of Upper and Lower Egypt,
Daughter of Ra, Whom Her Heart Loves,
One from Ta-Sety,
Her seat is where Wepeset stands,
While She is angry,
When She comes from Bugem.[181]

---

[181] Inconnu-Bocquillon, Danielle, *Le mythe de la déesse lointaine à Philae*, *BdE 132*, (Le Caire/Cairo: IFAO, 2001), 92.

HYMN OF TEFNUT

Tefnut, Daughter of Ra,
Who resides in the Abaton,
One who burns the enemies of Her Father Ra,
Who protects His majesty daily,
And unites with Him in Senmet.[182]

---

[182] Inconnu-Bocquillon, Danielle, *Le mythe de la déesse lointaine à Philae, BdE 132*, (Le Caire/Cairo: IFAO, 2001), 93.

HYMN OF TEFNUT

Tefnut, Daughter of Ra,
Who resides in the Abaton,
August and Powerful,
Regent of Philae,
One who comes from Kenset to Egypt,
And makes Her seat in Senmet,
In the company of Her brother.[183]

---

[183] Inconnu-Bocquillon, Danielle, *Le mythe de la déesse lointaine à Philae, BdE 132*, (Le Caire/Cairo: IFAO, 2001), 97.

HYMN OF TEFNUT

Tefnut, Daughter of Ra,
Uraeus of Ra, Lady of the Abaton,
Regent and Lady of Philae,
Mistress of the Sky,
Regent of All the Gods.[184]

---

[184] Inconnu-Bocquillon, Danielle, *Le mythe de la déesse lointaine à Philae, BdE 132,* (Le Caire/Cairo: IFAO, 2001), 101.

HYMN OF TEFNUT

Tefnut, Daughter of Ra,
Who resides in the Abaton,
August and Powerful,
One Who springs from Kenset,
Tefnut, Daughter of Ra,
Who resides in the Abaton,
August and Powerful,
One Who springs from Kenset,
Coming toward Senmet,
In the form of Wepeset,
Tefnut, Daughter of Ra,
Lady of Senmet,
Regent and Lady of Philae.[185]

---

[185] Inconnu-Bocquillon, Danielle, *Le mythe de la déesse lointaine à Philae, BdE 132*, (Le Caire/Cairo: IFAO, 2001), 109.

HYMN OF TEFNUT

Tefnut, Daughter of Ra,
Who resides in the Abaton,
Tefnut, Daughter of Ra,
Who resides in the Abaton,
Wepeset, Venerable, Lady of Senmet,
Tefnut, Daughter of Ra,
Who resides in the Abaton,
Wepeset, Venerable, Lady of Senmet.[186]

---

[186] Inconnu-Bocquillon, Danielle, *Le mythe de la déesse lointaine à Philae, BdE 132*, (Le Caire/Cairo: IFAO, 2001), 113.

HYMN OF TEFNUT

Tefnut, Daughter of Ra,
Who resides in the Abaton,
Venerable, *Uraeus*,
Lady of Senmet,
Eye of Ra, Mistress of the Sky,
Regent of All the Gods.[187]

---

[187] Inconnu-Bocquillon, Danielle, *Le mythe de la déesse lointaine à Philae, BdE 132*, (Le Caire/Cairo: IFAO, 2001), 114.

HYMN OF TEFNUT

Tefnut, Daughter of Ra,
Who resides in the Abaton,
August and Perfect,
Lady of Philae,
Sovereign in Senmet,
Tefnut, Daughter of Ra,
Who resides in the Abaton,
August and Perfect,
Lady of Philae,
Sovereign in Senmet,
Tefnut, Daughter of Ra,
Who resides in the Abaton.[188]

---

[188] Inconnu-Bocquillon, Danielle, *Le mythe de la déesse lointaine à Philae, BdE 132*, (Le Caire/Cairo: IFAO, 2001), 117.

HYMN OF TEFNUT

Tefnut, Daughter of Ra in Philae,
Great Flame Goddess in Senmet.[189]

---

[189] Kockelmann, Holger and Erich Winter, *Philae III: Die Zweite Ostkolonnade des Tempels der Isis in Philae. (CO II und CO II K)*, (Verlag der Osterreichischen Akademie der Wissenschaften/Austrian Academy of Sciences, 2016), 141.

HYMN OF TEFNUT

Tefnut, Daughter of Ra, Lady of the Abaton
In whose vicinity is the Great Flame
One Who Burns with Fire, Dwelling in Elephantine
And appears in Senmet for all eternity.[190]

---

[190] Kockelmann, Holger and Erich Winter, *Philae III: Die Zweite Ostkolonnade des Tempels der Isis in Philae. (CO II und CO II K)*, (Verlag der Osterreichischen Akademie der Wissenschaften/Austrian Academy of Sciences, 2016), 189.

HYMN OF TEFNUT

Tefnut,
Daughter of Ra on the Abaton,
Great Flame Goddess.[191]

---

[191] Kockelmann, Holger and Erich Winter, *Philae III: Die Zweite Ostkolonnade des Tempels der Isis in Philae. (CO II und CO II K)*, (Verlag der Osterreichischen Akademie der Wissenschaften/Austrian Academy of Sciences, 2016), 231.

HYMN OF TEFNUT

Tefnut,
Uraeus Snake,
Princess of Life, the House of Birth
She cleans Her city for Her son Heru.[192]

---

[192] Kockelmann, Holger and Erich Winter, *Philae III: Die Zweite Ostkolonnade des Tempels der Isis in Philae. (CO II und CO II K)*, (Verlag der Osterreichischen Akademie der Wissenschaften/Austrian Academy of Sciences, 2016), 263.

Hymn of Tefnut

Tefnut, Daughter of Ra
In the midst of the Abaton,
Eye of Ra,
Uraeus on His Forehead.[193]

---

[193] Kockelmann, Holger and Erich Winter, *Philae III: Die Zweite Ostkolonnade des Tempels der Isis in Philae. (CO II und CO II K)*, (Verlag der Osterreichischen Akademie der Wissenschaften/Austrian Academy of Sciences, 2016), 292.

Excerpt Hymn of Tefnut

Let Tefnut
Awake in Peace, with You,
In Her name of Menhyt-Nebetuu
Two Birds of Ra being united in one Being,
It is Nit, the Divine Mother of Ra,
Who created Your bodies,
It is She who nourishes Your flesh with Her milk.[194]

---

[194] Sauneron, Serge, *Esna V: Les fêtes religieuses d'Esna aux derniers siècles du paganisme*, (Cairo: IFAO, 1962; 2004), 89. Within a hymn to Khnum. Translated by Chelsea Bolton.

AWAKEN HYMN TO SHU AND TEFNUT

Shu and Tefnut,
Awaken in Peace!
Awaken Peacefully!
May the Two Birds of Ra,
Awaken in Peace!
Awaken Peacefully!
May the Two Children of Atum,
Awaken in Peace!
Awaken Peacefully!
Awake, the Two Children as Eyes
In Peace, Awaken Peacefully!
Let the Lion and Lioness, Awaken!
Ancestor Gods,
Son of Tatenen, Born of Ra,
Atum and His Two Birds,
Flood together with the Grassland,
In their names of Khnum and Nebetuu,
the Great Gods who are Your Ka,
United with Your bodies,
Let the Mother of God awaken,
Peaceful with You
And She does not depart from You,
Ever![195]

---

[195] Sauneron, Serge, *Esna V: Les fêtes religieuses d'Esna aux derniers siècles du paganisme*, (Cairo: IFAO, 1962; 2004), 90. Excerpt from a hymn. Translated by Chelsea Bolton.

EPILOGUE

Bibliography

Bryan, Betsy M, "Hatshepsut and Cultic Revelries in the New Kingdom." *Creativity and Innovation in the Reign of Hatshepsut,* SAOC 69 (2014): 93-123.

Cauville, Sylvie, *Le Temple de Dendara : La Porte d'Isis, Dendara,* Cairo: IFAO, 1999.

El-Saghir, Mohamed and Dominique Valbelle. "Komir. I. - The Discovery of Komir Temple. Preliminary Report. II. - Deux hymnes aux divinités de Komir : Anoukis et Nephthys." BIFAO 83 (1983), p. 164-166.

Goyon, J.-Cl. *Confirmation du pouvoir royal au Nouvel An: Brooklyn Museum Papyrus 47.218.50, BdE 52,* Cairo: IFAO, 1972.

Inconnu-Bocquillon, Danielle, *Le mythe de la déesse lointaine à Philae, BdE 132,* Le Caire/Cairo: IFAO, 2001.

Junker, Hermann, *Der Grosse Pylon des Tempels der Isis in Phila,* Wien: Kommission bei Rudolf M. Rohrer, 1958.

Junker, Hermann and Erich Winter, *Das Geburtshaus des Tempels der Isis in Phila,* Wien: Kommissionsverlag H. Böhlaus Nachf., 1965.

Kockelmann, Holger and Erich Winter, *Philae III: Die Zweite Ostkolonnade des Tempels der Isis in Philae.* (CO II und CO II K), Verlag der Osterreichischen Akademie der Wissenschaften/Austrian Academy of Sciences, 2016.

Lesko, Barbara, *The Great Goddesses of Egypt.* University of Oklahoma Press, 1999.

Ouda, Ahmed M. Mekawy. "The Canopic Box of NS-'3-RWD (BM EA 8539)." *The Journal of Egyptian Archaeology 98, no. 1* (2012): 127-138.

Pinch, Geraldine, *Egyptian Mythology: A Guide to the Gods, Goddesses and Traditions of Ancient Egypt*, New York: Oxford University Press, 2004.

Richter, Barbara A., *The Theology of Hathor of Dendera: Aural and Visual Scribal Techniques in the Per-Wer Sanctuary*, Lockwood Press, 2016.

Richter, Barbara A., "On the Heels of the Wandering Goddess: The Myth and the Festival at the Temples of the Wadi el-Hallel and Dendera." Dolinska, Monika and Beinlich, Horst (eds.) 8 (2010): 155-186.

Rosenow, Daniela. "The Naos of 'Bastet, Lady of the Shrine' from Bubastis." *The Journal of Egyptian Archaeology* 94, no. 1 (January 2008): 247-66.

Sauneron, Serge, *Esna V: Les fêtes religieuses d'Esna aux derniers siècles du paganisme*, Cairo: IFAO, 1962; 2004.

Siuda, Tamara L., *The Ancient Egyptian Prayerbook*, Stargazer Design, 2009.

Siuda, Tamara L., *Nebt-Het: Lady of the House*, Stargazer Design, 2010.

Siuda, Tamara L., *The Ancient Egyptian Daybook*, Stargazer Design, 2016.

Stadler, Martin Andreas, *Théologie et culte au temple de Soknopaios: Etudes sur la Religion d'un Village Egyptien Pendant l'Epoque Romaine.*, Paris: Cybele, 2017.

Wilkinson, Richard H. *The Complete Gods and Goddesses of Ancient Egypt.* (New York: Thames and Hudson, 2003.

Ancient Artifacts

Canopic Chest Hymn to Nephthys from the Saite Period: British
Museum: Museum Number: EA8539

Glossary of Goddesses

Aset, Auset (Isis): Aset is a goddess of the throne, sovereignty, kingship, ancestral lineage and traditions, death, magic, healing, protection, and knowledge. She is the throne of kings, a goddess who governs over the authority of rulers and the sovereignty of kings. She is the faithful wife, who stayed married to Her husband even after his death. She is a devoted mother, who raised Her son, protecting him from dangerous forces and assisted him throughout his trials for Kingship. She is a trickster, using Her magic and guile to obtain the power of Ra's Name. She is a powerful sorceress, who halted the Sun Boat in order to heal Her son and who conceived an heir from Her dead husband. She is a compassionate healer, who cured a boy from a scorpion sting despite the transgressions of his mother. She is the Great of Magic, all magic and knowledge are hers to command for she knows all in Heaven and on Earth.

She is a cunning shape-shifter, a wily trickster, a powerful sorceress and a devoted wife and mother in the myths. She mourned her slain husband and raised Her son alone. She is the protector of Her brother, son and father.

She is the star Sopdet (Sirius) who heralded the Nile's flood, the New Year and the calculation of the festival calendar. She is the Goddess of every year and of sacred time. She is both a beneficial Goddess of rainfall and the terrifying Goddess of the torrential flood. As a protective Eye of Ra, She's the Goddess of the warmth of the sun and its scorching, fiery rays. Blue is the color of the fiercest fire and white is the brightest of lights; these are Her colors which aptly describe Her nature for She is both a fierce and bright goddess.

When her husband was slain, she searched with her sister, Nebet Het to find his body. Upon discovering the body, she found that it was in pieces. Aset searched for the pieces and put her husband back together. Using her magic, Aset fashioned a golden phallus for Wesir since his original one had been eaten by a fish in the Nile. With her magic, she was able to bring him back to life long enough to conceive an heir. Wesir then became the first mummy and the King of the Afterlife. Aset gave birth to her son, Heru-sa-Aset and helped him during his trials for the throne of Egypt.

She is the Goddess of the star Sopdet (Sirius) whose helical rising heralds the annual flood of the Nile. The rainstorms which flood the Nile at this time are said to be her tears shed for her slain husband. She is the Goddess of the fertility of plants.

As the Celestial Cow, she is the Creator Goddess, the Mother of Ra and the Goddess of the star-strewn sky. Aset is the Tree Goddess and the Lady of the Sycamore, when she nourishes the deceased. Aset is the Lady of the Underworld, the Queen of the Ancestors and Lady of the West (*Amenti*), which is the final resting place for the deceased.

Her sacred animals are the black kite, falcon, cow, female pig, female dog, lioness, leopard/panther, female hippopotamus, scorpion and cobra. She is the wife of Wesir and the mother of Heru-sa-Aset, Wepwawet, Yinepu, Sobek, Min and possibly, Sekhmet as the Daughter of Wesir. She is the daughter of Nut and Geb. She can also be the daughter of Ra or Tefnut. She is the sister of Nebet Het, Set, Heru Wer, and Wesir. Other forms of the goddess are: Aset-Sopdet, Aset-Serqet, Aset-Nebet Het, Aset-Seshat, Aset-Nut, Aset-Nit, Aset-Hethert and Aset-Sekhmet.

Bast (Bastet): Bast was depicted as a lioness headed woman. Like many other goddesses, Bast was an Eye of Ra, a solar goddess and the warrior and avenging lady. She was the goddess who left and returned to Egypt within the *Distant Goddess Myth*, like most other ancient Egyptian Goddesses. Like all other Eyes of Ra, Bast was appeased with an *Isheru-*

lake. She was also pacified with the sistrum-rattle and was offered the mirror and the Menat-necklace to calm her rage.

Later in Bast's history, she became associated with the domestic cat and had attributes such as the the Guardian of the Home and Granary and the Lady of Perfume, Beauty, Music, Joy and Dance. Bast is the Wife of Ra-Atum and the Mother of Heru *Hekenu* (Horus of Praises) in Per-Bast (Bubastis). Bast is also the Mother of Ma'ahes and Nefertem. There is a form of Bast joined with Mut called Bast-Mut worshipped as the Temple of Karnak. Other forms of the goddess are Bast-Sekhmet and Bast-Aset.

Hethert, (Hetharu; Hwt Hrw; Hathor): Hethert is the goddess of joy, love, beauty, motherhood, a creator goddess, a patron of the arts, music, dance and prosperity, a goddess who guards the dead and protector of the sun god. She is the Lady of the Underworld, Lady of the Sycamore and the Lady of West (*Amenti*); all are attributes of the Goddess of the Dead. She is associated with the Celestial Cow, the cobra or *Uraeus*, the lioness and the falcon. She is also associated with the *menat*-necklace, the papyrus scepter and the sistrum. She is the Distant Goddess who transforms into a raging lioness and is called back to Egypt by one of the other gods. She transforms back into Hethert and is placated with offerings with a procession along an *Isheru*-lake. Her husband is Heru Wer (Horus, the Elder) and her son is Ihy, the god of joy and the sistrum. She is the daughter, mother or wife of Ra. She was honored at the Temple of Karnak as Hethert-Mut. Other forms of the goddess are Hethert-Nut, Hethert-Tefnut and Hethert-Sekhmet.

Menhyt (Menhit): She is depicted as a lioness-headed woman whose name means "She Who Slaughters". She is a protective goddess associated with war, lionesses, the *Uraeus* and is an Eye of Ra. She is one of the goddesses within the Myth of the Distant Goddess. At Esna, she was the wife of Khnum and the mother of Heka, the god of magic. Other forms of the goddess are Menhyt-Nit and Mehnyt-Sekhmet.

Mut (Muth): She is a creator goddess, a protector goddess and a goddess associated with royal power, kingship, male kings and female kings. She the Celestial Cow: the Creator Goddess, the Mother of Ra and the Lady of the Night Sky. She is a goddess associated with protection, magic, family and motherhood. She is the queenly mother, a stately lady and a protector of the state. She is the Lady of the Sky and the Earth. She is an Eye of Ra and is appeased at the *Isheru*-lake. Her sacred animals are the cat, the lioness, the cobra and the cow. She is the wife of Amun or Amun-Ra and the Mother of Khonsu. At Karnak, Mut took on the form of other goddesses and these forms were said to be aspects of Mut: Mut-Hethert, Mut-Sekhmet, Mut-Aset and Mut-Bast.

Nebet Het (Nebt-Het; Nephthys): Her name Nebet Het can be translated to "Lady or Mistress of the Palace, Temple, Tomb or Home". As Lady of the Palace, She is the protector of the King, the King's residence and the mother of Heru. As the Lady of the House or Temple, She governs over holy places such as temples and shrines as a guard who protects against impurities. As the Lady of the Home, She governs over the household: its occupants and upkeep. As Lady of the Tomb, She is the goddess over burial and the remembrance of the dead.

As the second wife and mourner of Wesir, Nebet Het is the goddess of the inundation of the Nile, the rainfall, and the fertility of crops. She is a Goddess of the Underworld who helps the dead transform. As the wife of Set, She is a war-like Goddess, the goddess of the edges of the desert and an averter of evil forces.

She is often paired with her sister Aset (Isis) in various roles and functions such as an Eye of Ra and Great of Magic; a protector of the shrines and temples; and a mourner and wife of Wesir. Together the Two Sisters bring the rain for the Nile's flood, bring the sunrise and sunset, are mothers of Heru and Yinepu (Anubis), are averters of evil and protect the Gods: Ra, Heru and Wesir. They are associated with the afterlife with the titles: Lady of the Underworld, Lady of the Sycamore and Lady of the West (*Amenti*).

Not much is known about Nebet Het outside of the Wesir mythos or Her association with her sister Aset. She does have two epithets which describe two aspects of her character: *Kherseket* (She Who Wipes Away Tears) and *Merkhetes* (She Whose Flame is Painful). She is the goddess who comforts those who suffer and is the fierce protective deity who destroys enemies with flame.

Her sacred animals are the cobra, leopard, lioness, female black kite, female dog, female donkey, ibis and hippopotamus. She is the wife of Ra and the mother of Yinepu. She is the consort of Wesir and the mother of Heru. She is the mother of a daughter by Heru Hemen. She is the wife of Set and had a child with him, possibly Yinepu. She is the daughter of Nut, Geb or Ra. She is the sister of Aset, Heru Wer, Set and Wesir. Other forms of the goddess can take are: Nebet Het-Aset, Nebet Het-Seshat, Nebet Het-Nit and Nebet Het-Anuket.

Nit (Neith): Nit is depicted as a woman wearing either of these two headdresses: the Red Crown of Lower Egypt or a shield with two crossed arrows. She is an ancient Egyptian goddess who was associated with early dynastic queens via their names. She is a goddess associated with hunting, war, the creation of the world and as a guide and guard of the dead. She is like Wepwawet in that she is an Opener of the Way and has the epithet the Female Wepwawet. She has an aspect as the Celestial Cow who is the creator goddess, the Mother of Ra and a guide to the deceased. She created the world with her words. She is also an Eye of Ra, a Daughter of Ra and a fierce lioness within the Myth of the Distant Goddess. She is the consort of Set and the Mother or Daughter of Sobek.[196] Nit is called the "Father of Fathers and Mother of Mothers" as a creator deity, emphasizing a more androgynous nature.[197]

---

[196] Stadler, Martin Andreas, *Théologie et culte au temple de Soknopaios: Etudes sur la Religion d'un Village Egyptien Pendant l'Epoque Romaine*, (Paris: Cybele, 2017), 66.

[197] Lesko, Barbara, *The Great Goddesses of Egypt*, (Oklahoma: University of Oklahoma Press, 1999), 61.

Her sacred animals are the lioness, cobra, cow and the bee. Other forms of the goddess are Nit-Menhyt, Nit-Nebet Het, Nit-Anuket and Nit-Nut.

Nut (Nuit): She is normally depicted as a naked woman dappled with stars and outstretched over the Earth, personified by her husband Geb. She is also depicted as a naked woman with the journey of the sun shown throughout her body. In iconography, she is shown as a clothed woman with three headdresses: a small *nw* pot on her head, the headdress of the sundisk in between the cow horns and the Hathor crown with the *nw* pot above it. The *nw* pot is the hieroglyph for her name.

Nut is the goddess of the sky. During the day, Ra travels through the Heavens and at night, Nut is the sky filled with stars which represent the ancestors. As the night sky, she is the place where the dead reside. One of her titles is *Amenti* or Lady of the West, which is the Land of the Ancestors. She also nourishes the deceased as the Tree Goddess or Lady of the Sycamore.

As the sky, Nut births Ra every morning at dawn and devours him every night at sunset so he can embark on his nightly underworld journey.

She is both the bright goddess of stars and the mysterious Veil of Heaven. She is an Eye of Ra within the Myth of the Distant Goddess. She is the Celestial Cow, the Creator Goddess, the Mother of Ra and the Goddess of the Stars.

In one myth, at the beginning of creation, Nut and Geb were born. The two fell in love instantly. But to make way for creation, they had to be separated. But Nut was pregnant with children fathered by Geb. So, Nut became the sky and Geb became the earth below. All of creation lies between them. Rain can be said to be Nut's tears as she mourns her separation from Geb.

In another myth, when Nut became pregnant, Ra forbade her to give birth on any day of the year. So Djehuty won a few extra days beyond the 360 day year from the moon god, Khonsu and the 5 extra days were created. She gave birth to the gods and goddesses, one on each day: Wesir, Heru Wer, Set, Aset, and Nebet Het.

In another myth, Nut (or Hethert-Nut) turns into the lioness goddess Sekhmet and on Ra's orders, slays evil humans who were rebelling against Ra. Once Nut-Sekhmet's rage is appeased, she turns back into the Heavenly Cow. Ra asks her to ascend with him to the sky. Once high enough, Ra says he will watch over all the people. Nut needs the strength to withstand such a height. So Ra makes stars. Nut is now the star-filled sky who watches over creation. With this myth, the Underworld portrayed as Nut's star-filled sky was created and so death entered the world. Nut is the Heavenly Mother and Lady of the Underworld.

She is associated with water, the Nile, the Milky Way, rainfall and thunder.

Nut's sacred animals are the cow, the female pig, the female hippopotamus, the pufferfish, the lioness, the cobra/snake, and the vulture. She is the Daughter of Shu and Tefnut or the Daughter of Ra. She is the Wife of Geb and Mother of Aset, Nebet Het, Set, Heru Wer and Wesir. She can also be the Mother of Ra and Wepwawet. Other forms of the goddess are Nut-Aset, Nut-Hethert, Nut-Mut and Nut-Nit.

Sekhmet (Sachmis): Sekhmet means "Powerful One". She is depicted as a lioness headed woman with headdress of the solar disk with the *uraeus*. She is the goddess of healing, surgeons, an averter of disease, the sun, flame, integrity, appropriate action, protection, war and magic. She is an Eye of Ra whose rage was appeased at the *Isheru* lake of some temples. She is the Celestial Cow, who is the creator goddess, the mother of Ra and the lady of the stars at night. She is associated with the lioness, cobra, and the cow. She is the wife of Ptah and the mother of Nefertem, Ma'ahes and Imhotep. Other forms of the goddess are Sekhmet-Hethert, Sekhmet-Aset, Sekhmet-Tefnut, Sekhmet-Nut and Sekhmet-Nit.

Serqet (Serket; Selket; Selkis): Serqet's full name is *Serqet-hetyt* which means "She who causes the throat to breathe".[198] Serqet is depicted as a woman with a scorpion on her head, or in the form of one of her sacred animals. Sometimes Serqet was shown as a woman crowned with a non-venomous water scorpion to emphasize her beneficial attributes.[199] Serqet is associated with the dead as a protector of the canopic jars, a protector of the deceased, as a deity associated with the embalming chamber and as a guardian within the Underworld. Scorpions were seen as a "symbol of motherhood" since they carry their young on their backs. One of her epithets is "Divine Mother." Alternatively, Serqet can be viewed as a deity who wards off the scorpion's poison or even the one who causes it. Like Aset, Serqet is a goddess of magic, medicine and healing, especially getting rid of toxins, such as scorpion stings. Serqet is a guardian, a protector, a magician, a medicine woman and a Lady of Healing.

There is a form of the goddess called Aset-Serqet who was depicted as a woman with a scorpion on her head; this form of the goddess was honored in Nubia. Aset-Serqet is thought of as a fusion of the goddesses or Aset as the scorpion goddess. Serqet may have been assimilated into the worship of Aset as another form of the multi-faceted goddess.

Serqet is a Daughter of Ra, and Eye of Ra and is associated with the *Distant Goddess myth*. She protects Ra and the Sun Boat during the nightly journey through the Underworld. She is the mother of the snake-headed god, Nehebkau.

Her sacred animals are the scorpion, lioness and the cobra. Serqet's other forms include: Serqet-Aset and Serqet-Nebet Het.

Seshat (Sefkhet Abwy): Seshat is the patron goddess of writing, architecture, mathematics, astrology, astronomy, record-keeping, book-

---

198Wilkinson, Richard H. *The Complete Gods and Goddesses of Ancient Egypt*. (New York: Thames and Hudson, 2003), 234.

199Pinch, Geraldine. *Egyptian Mythology: A Guide to the Gods, Goddesses and Traditions of Ancient Egypt*. (New York: Oxford University Press, 2004), 189.

keeping, building, knowledge and libraries. She is the patron of the "stretching of the cord" ritual which was done before temples were built. She is often depicted as a woman wearing a panther-skin dress, holding a stylus and reed pen. The spots of the panther represent stars and the night sky; this association makes Seshat the goddess of time, astronomy and the dead. Her head is adorned with a seven-pointed star with two horns pointed downward. The two horns used to be a crescent moon. She is often the daughter or wife of Djehuty (Thoth). Seshat can be a creator deity who created the world through her words and was called the "Female Creator".[200] Seshat's sacred animals are the cobra and leopard/panther. Other forms the goddess are: Seshat-Aset, Seshat-Hethert and Seshat-Nebet Het.

Tefnut (Tefenet): Tefnut is the Daughter of Ra and the Sister and Wife of Shu, the god of wind and light. Tefnut is one of the goddesses in the *Distant Goddess myth*, an Eye of Ra, a fierce lioness and is placated with offerings at a processional with an *Isheru*-lake. In one creation myth, she is created by Ra-Atum or Atum as his first daughter, along with Shu as his first son. Tefnut is the goddess of the sun, the solar Eye, moisture and rainfall. Tefnut is the Mother of Nut and Geb and the Grandmother to all of Nut's children. She can be depicted as a lioness or as a lioness headed woman with a *uraeus* or with a sundisk and *uraeus* on top of her head. Her sacred animals are the lioness and the cobra. Other forms of the goddess are Tefnut-Mut, Tefnut-Aset, Tefnut-Sekhmet and Tefnut-Hethert.

---

[200] Adapted from a translation by Barbara A. Richter in Richter, Barbara A., *The Theology of Hathor of Dendera: Aural and Visual Scribal Techniques in the Per-Wer Sanctuary*, (Lockwood Press, 2016), 278.

Glossary

- Abu: (Greek: Elephantine) Khnum's sacred city on the First Cataract of the Nile.
- Abdju: (Modern: Abydos) The sacred city of Wesir and the place of the burial site of the first ancient Egyptian kings.
- Akh (s)/Akhu (p): the ancestors, beloved dead.
- Alexandria: A metropolitan port city in the Ptolemaic period where Aset (Isis) was honored in the Lighthouse of Alexandria on Pharos Island.
- Amenti: An alternative name for the Duat. The name comes from the Goddess Amentet, the Lady of the West. She is the Goddess of the sunset, the night sky, the deceased and the Underworld. *Amenti* is a title and manifestation of the Goddesses Aset, Hethert, Nebet Het and Nut.
- Amun-Ra: A syncretic deity who rose to prominence in the New Kingdom. He was a combination of Amun and Ra. Amun-Ra is the husband of Mut and father of Khonsu.
- Anuket: (Greek: Anukis) A Goddess associated with the Nile's inundation and whose sacred animal is the gazelle. Anuket was associated with the Nile as the waters receded while Satet was associated with the Nile as the waters rose. She was worshiped at Elephantine along with Satet and Khnum and at Komir she shared a temple with Nebet Het.
- Aset: (also Auset; Greek: Isis) A Goddess of authority, sovereignty and kings. She is the Goddess of magic par excellence who knows Ra's secret name. She is a solar Eye of Ra who wards off enemies from her husband, son and the sun God. On the Night Boat, Aset wards off Apep with her magic.

She heralds the New Year rising in the sky as the star Sopdet.
She is the wife of Wesir and the mother of Heru-sa-Aset.

- Antinoe: (Greek: Antinopolis) Ancient city dedicated to
  Antinious, the deified lover of the Roman Emperor Hadrian
  who drowned in the Nile.
- Ba (s)/Bau (p): The eternal essence of a being, the soul.
  The *ba* of a deity went into the cult statues and other
  theophanies were the manifestations of the deity on earth. A
  physical manifestation of a deity such as a cult statue, an animal
  or a natural force. The *ba* of a human is an eternal part of the
  soul.
- Bast: (Greek: Bastet) A lioness Goddess who protects her father
  Ra, is an avenging Eye of Ra and is a Goddess of the yearly solar
  cycle. She is also a Goddess of joy and music like Hethert. In
  later periods, she became more associated with the domestic
  housecat.
- Behdet: (Greek: Apollonopolis Magna; Modern: Edfu) The city
  and temple are sacred to Heru Wer or Horus the Elder.
- Djedet: (Greek: Mendes) City sacred to the fish Goddess
  Hatmehyt and her consort, Banebdjedet.
- Djehuty: (Greek: Thoth) The ibis or baboon headed God of
  time, wisdom, math, science, scribes, recordkeeping and the
  moon. In some inscriptions, Djehuty is the father or son of Aset.
- Dua: This word means praise or worship.
- Duat: This word means the sunrise, praise or worship, and the
  "Underworld". This is the Another name for this place
  is *Amenti*.
- Geb: The earth God associated with the land itself and all that
  grows upon it. He is associated with all the minerals in the
  earth. He is associated with the dead since the dead are buried
  in the earth. In the beginning, he was separated from his wife,
  Nut so that the earth and sky could be created. He is the father
  of Aset, Nebet Het, Set, Wesir and Heru Wer.

- Gebtu: (Greek: Koptos or Coptos; Modern: Qift) A town sacred to Min, Aset, Wesir and Heru-sa-Aset.
- Hebyt: (also Per-Hebitet; Greek: Isiopolis; currently Behbeit el-Hagar) An ancient sacred city of Aset. The ancient Egyptian name of this city means "House of the Festive Goddess". Her temple in this city is called the Iseion or Temple of Isis in Greek.
- Heka: (literally, "magic"). A God and a concept. The concept is a force of energy that resides in all things, which can be manipulated by deities and humans. It has been translated as magic, but it is really the power of the *ka* (life force) in motion.
- Hekau: A magician, a sorceror or sorceress, one who uses heka; also a plural form of *heka*, "magic".
- Heru pa Khered: (Greek: Harpokrates; Horus the Child) A form of Heru-sa-Aset who is a child. He and his mother are mentioned together in many healing spells.
- Heru nedj itef: (Greek: Harendotes; Horus, Savior of His Father) The form of Heru-sa-Aset who has battled Set and won the throne of Egypt. He has inherited the throne of his father.
- Heru-sa-Aset: (Greek: Harsiese; Horus son of Isis) The son of Aset and Wesir who can manifest in many forms such as a child, a warrior battling Set for the throne and a triumphant King. He is the God of kingship and proficient in magical spells because of his mother. He is a God of strength, leadership and community. He is often portrayed as a hawk headed God with the Double Crown.
- Heru-sema-tawy: (Greek: Harsomtus; Horus the Uniter of the Two Lands) A form of Heru the Child who is the son of Hethert and Heru-Wer.
- Heru Wer: (Greek: Haroeris; Horus the Elder) The sky God of kings, and communities whose eyes are the sun and the moon. He is a protector and a warrior. He is the twin brother of Set, uncle of Heru-sa-Aset and the brother of Aset, Wesir and Nebet

Het. He is often portrayed as a falcon headed God with the White Crown.

- Hethert: (also Hetharu; Greek: Hathor) A joyous Goddess of beauty, love, and fertility. She is an Eye of Ra and an avenging solar deity. She is also a Goddess who protects the dead.
- Het-Ka-Ptah: (also Mennefer; Memphis) The sacred city of the craftsman God Ptah. The name means "House of the Ka of Ptah".
- Hypostasis: a distinct, seperate aspect within a unified God.
- Imet: (currently known as Tell Nabasha) A city that was sacred to Wadjet.
- Iunet: (currently known as Dendera) The sacred city of the Goddess Hethert.
- Iunu: (also On; Greek: Heliopolis) The sacred city of Ra and the Gods of his creation myth. The Ennead of this city consisted of Ra, Shu, Tefnut, Nut, Geb, Wesir, Aset, Nebet Het, Set and Heru Wer.
- Ka (s)/Kau (p): The vital essence of a person or deity; the collective vital essence of a family line or kingly lineage; magic.
- Khent-min: (also Ipu or Apu; Greek: Chemmis or Panopolis; currently Akhmim) A city sacred to Min. In the Wesir Mythos, Aset takes her son to the marshes here to raise.
- Khmun (Greek: Hermopolis) The sacred city of Djehuty.
- Khnum: A Ram-headed God of the Nile's inundation, potters and a master craftsman. He creates the *kau* of humans on his potter's wheel. Khnum is also one of the creators of the world.
- Ma'at: (Greek: Mayet) A Goddess and the concept of truth, order and balance of the universe.
- Menat: (also Menet) A necklace used like a rattle in ritual, especially the Goddesses.
- Mehet Weret: (also Celestial Cow; Greek: Methyer) The cow Goddess of the primeval waters, creation, the birth of the sun God and the heavenly sky. She is the caretaker of the dead since

the stars fill the night sky. She is a manifestation of Nut, Nit, Nebet Het, Mut, Hethert and Aset.

- Min: The ithyphallic God of fertility and procreation. Aset can be paired with him as her consort or her son.
- Mut: A Goddess of sovereignty, royalty and an Eye of Ra. The wife of Amun-Ra and mother of Khonsu.
- Nebet Het: (Greek: Nephthys) Her name can mean Lady of the House, Lady of the Temple or Lady of the Tomb. She is a Goddess who protects boundaries such as the sacred from the profane or twilight lands during dawn and dusk. As a solar Goddess, she is an Eye of Ra and a protector of Ra and Wesir. She weeps with Aset causing the flooding of the Nile. In some myths, Yinepu is her son. She can be a consort of Set, Ra or Wesir.
- Nefertem: (also Nefertum) A patron God of scents and fragrances, Nefertem is a God associated with the lotus and wears on upon his head. He also can be depicted as a child sitting on a lotus flower. He wards off evil in his leonine form. He is the son of Sekhmet and Ptah. He is also considered the son of Bast.
- Nekheb: (currently known as El-Kab) This is the sacred city of the vulture Goddess Nekhbet.
- Nekhen: (Greek: Hierakonpolis) City sacred to Heru of Nekhen, the God Khnum and the Goddess Nit.
- Nit: (Greek: Neith) The tutelary Goddess of Lower Egypt. She wears the Red Crown and holds bows and arrows. She is a primordial Goddess who began creation. She has a manifestation as the celestial cow where she is a creator deity, the lady of the primeval ocean and the night sky, holding the dead. She is a Goddess associated with protection of the dead as she protects one of the canopic jars. She is a mother of Sobek and a consort of Set.

- Nut: The Goddess of the night sky filled with stars. She is the Goddess of the dead as their mother and caretaker. She gives birth to the sun God each morning and devours him each evening. As the celestial cow, she is the Goddess of the primeval waters and the dead. She is the mother of Aset, Nebet Het, Set, Wesir and Heru Wer.
- Of Iunu: (Greek: Heliopolitan; of Heliopolis) This is normally translated as the Heliopolitan or the one of Heliopolis or the city of Iunu in Ancient Egyptian.
- Per Bast: (Greek: Bubastis) The sacred city of the Goddess Bast.
- Per Hethert: (also Tpyhwt; Greek: Aphroditopolis; Modern: Atfih) A city sacred to Hethert.
- Per Medjed: (Greek: Oxyrhynchus) A city sacred to Wepwawet during the New Kingdom (along with Aset and Hethert).
- Per Wesir: (also Djedu; Greek: Busiris) This city was sacred to Wesir.
- Pesdjet: (Greek: Ennead) A group of deities important to cities; this number could consist of nine deities, but it was not limited to that number.
- Pharos Island: A small island in the city of Alexandria where a lighthouse once stood as one of the Seven Wonders of the World. Aset of Pharos (Isis Pharia) was honored here as its patron Goddess.
- Pilak: (also P'aaleq; Greek: Philae) The sacred temple and island of Aset during the Late through the Roman period. The temple was relocated to Agilkia Island due to the construction of the Aswan Dam.
- Ptah: A creator God of Memphis who is the divine patron of craftsmen. He is the consort of Sekhmet and father of Nefertem.
- Ra: (also Re) The sun God who created the world and who rules among the Gods as their King. He is the father of many Gods and Goddesses, including Aset. Ra is one of the Gods associated

with kingship and is often portrayed as a man with the head of a hawk wearing a solar disk.

- Ra Heruakhety: (Greek: Ra Horakhty; Ra-Horus of the Two Horizons) A fusion of the sun God Ra and Heru Wer. He represents the sun's journey both by day and night. He is often portrayed as a man with a falcon's head with a solar disk for his crown.

- Renenutet: (Greek: Thermuthis or Hermouthis) A cobra-headed Goddess of the harvest and the protection of granaries, associated with fate and childbirth and a protective Eye of Ra Goddess who destroys enemies. She is the consort of either Sobek or Geb and the mother of Nehebkau.

- Satet: (Greek: Satis) A tutelary Goddess of Elephantine and the Nile's waters. She wears the White Crown encased in antelope horns. Her consort is Khnum and her daughter is Anuket. She can be syncretized with Aset.

- Shedet: (Greek: Crocodilopolis; Modern: Dime or Faiyum) The marshes sacred to the crocodile God Sobek. Aset, Wesir and Heru-sa-Aset were worshipped alongside Sobek in this nome from the Middle Kingdom through the Roman period.

- Shu: The primordial God of air and sunlight. He is the consort of Tefnut and father of Nut and Geb. He is often portrayed as a man wearing an ostrich feather headdress or in leonine form.

- Sekhmet: (Greek: Sachmis) A lioness-headed Goddess who is the patron of healing and illness using magic and medicine to cure disease. As a daughter of Ra, she protects her father from evil forces. Like many Goddesses, she is an Eye of Ra. She is a protector and a warrior who defends ma'at. She is the patron of healers and surgeons. She is the mother of Nefertem and her consort is the creator God Ptah.

- Senem: (Greek: Abaton; currently Bigeh) An island nearby the Temple of Philae. Aset would honor Wesir during weekly processions to a temple here.

- Serqet: (also Selket; Greek: Selkis) A scorpion Goddess known for her healing abilities.
- Seshat: The Goddess of writing, scribes, record-keeping and recording the lives of kings. She was the patron of the "stretching the cord" ritual before a temple was built. As the tutelary Goddess of scribes, she is often depicted holding scribal implements. She is often depicted wearing a leopard skin over her attire and her head is adorned with a seven pointed palmette with a two bovine horns pointing downward.
- Set: (also Seth) The God of storms, the desert, foreigners, outsiders and strength. He guarded Ra's bark and killed Apep. In some myths, he is also the one who slays Wesir and challenges Heru-sa-Aset for the throne.
- Shai: (Greek: Psais; Agathos Daimon) The God of fate, fortune and destiny.
- Sobek: (Greek: Suchos) The crocodile God of the Nile waters, protection, strength and the sun. In some locations such as the Faiyum, Sobek is the son of Aset and Wesir.
- Sopdet: (Greek: Sothis; today known as Sirius) A form of Aset who brings the Nile's inundation and heralds the New Year as She rises in the sky. As the star Sopdet, Aset follows Wesir (Orion) in the sky.
- Swenett: (Greek: Syene; Modern: Aswan or Assuan) A trade-city nearby Philae sacred to the Goddess that the city was named for.
- Syncretic Deities: Two deities who have fused to make a third, separate deity which still contains the uniqueness of the two deities such as Aset-Tayet, Aset-Nut and Aset-Mut.
- Tayet: (also Tait) A deity of purification and the linen wrappings of the dead. She can be syncretized with or considered an aspect of Aset.
- Ta-senet (also Iunyt; Greek: Latopolis or Letopolis; Modern: Esna) A city sacred to Khnum and Nit.

- Tefnut: A lioness Goddess who is an Eye of Ra and associated with the force of moisture. She is a primordial deity as she was the first Goddess Ra created. She is the mother of Nut and the grandmother of Aset and her siblings.
- Tjebu: (Greek: Antinopolis) City sacred to Set.
- *Uraeus*: The fiery cobra who protects the sun God, whose solar power is destructive toward enemies and protective for everyone else. All Goddesses (and a few Gods) with the epithet Eye of Ra are associated with this cobra.
- Wadjet: (Greek: Buto) The patron Goddess of Lower Egypt. She is depicted as a *Uraeus* or a cobra headed woman. She is associated with royalty and protection. She is also an Eye of Ra.
- Waset: (Greek: Thebes) The sacred city of Amun, Mut and Khonsu during the New Kingdom and after.
- Wepwawet: (also, Upuaut; Greek: Ophois) A jackal God who is the Opener of the Way; he paves the way for armies, childbirth, the sunrise, rituals to the Gods and for the dead to cross over. He is associated with the wolf by the Greeks. He is a son of Aset.
- Wesir: (Greek: Osiris)-the God of vegetation and the king of the afterlife. Aset and Nebet Het mourn him after he is slain by Set. In some myths, he drowns in the Nile. Aset and Nebet Het search for him, find his body and bury it. Wesir is the father of Heru-sa-Aset.
- Yinepu: (Greek: Anubis) The jackal-headed God of embalming, a psychopomp for the deceased and a guardian of tombs. Depending on the myth, the son or adopted son of Aset.
- Zau: (Greek: Sais) The sacred city of the Goddess Nit.
- Zawty: (Greek: Lykopolis; currently known as Asyut) The sacred city of Wepwawet.

Gods and Goddesses Name List

- Aset, Auset (Isis)
- Bast, Bastet (Ubastis, Bubastis)
- Djehuty, Tehuti (Thoth)
- Hethert, Hetharu, Hwt Hrw (Hathor)
- Heru-pa-Khered (Horus, the Child; Harpocrates)
- Heru-sa-Aset (Horus, son of Isis; Horus, the Younger; Harsiese)
- Heru Wer (Horus, the Great; Horus, the Elder)
- Menhyt (Menhit)
- Mut (Mout; Muth)
- Nebet Het, Nebt-Het, Nebet Hwt (Nephthys)
- Nebetuu (Nebtu)
- Nit, Net (Neith)
- Nut (Nuit)
- Ra, Re
- Ra Heruakhety (Ra Horakhty)
- Sekhmet (Sachmis)
- Serqet, Serket, Selket (Selkis)
- Seshat, Seshet, Sesheta (Sefkhet Abwy)
- Sopdet (Sothis; Sirius)
- Tefnut (Tefenet)
- Wepwawet, Upuaut (Ophois)
- Wesir, Asar, Ausar (Osiris)
- Yinepu, Anpu, Inpu (Anubis)

Place Name List

- Abaton (Temple of Osiris on Bigeh Island near Philae)
- Abdju (Abydos)
- Bugem (Nubia)
- Djedu (Busiris in Lower Egypt)
- Pilak (Philae)
- Iatdi (Temple of Isis at Dendera)
- Iunet (Tentyris; Dendera)
- Iunu (Heliopolis)
- Kenset (Keneset; Bigeh)
- Khem (Letopolis)
- Per Bast (Bubastis)
- Per-Meru (Komir)
- Per Wesir (Busiris in Middle Egypt; Abusir)
- Senmet (Senmut; Elephantine)
- Tpyhwt (Busiris; Aphroditopolis; Atfih)
- Ta-Senet (Latopolis; Esna)
- Zawty (Lycopolis; Asyut)

About the Author

Chelsea Luellon Bolton has a BA and MA in Religious Studies from the University of South Florida. She is the author of *Lady of Praise, Lady of Power: Ancient Hymns of the Goddess Aset; Queen of the Road: Poetry of the Goddess Aset;* and *Magician, Mother and Queen: A Research Paper on the Goddess Aset.* Her other books are *Lord of Strength and Power: Ancient Hymns for Wepwawet* and *Sun, Star and Desert Sand: Poems for the Egyptian Gods.* She is the editor and a contributor of this anthology *She Who Speaks Through Silence: An Anthology for Nephthys.* Her other latest book is *Mother of Magic: Ancient Hymns for Aset.* Her current project is *Lady of the Temple: Ancient Hymns for Nephthys.* Her poetry has been previously published in various anthologies. She lives with tons of books and her anti-social feline companion. You can find more of her work at her blog address: http://fiercelybrightone.com

Website:
https://fiercelybrightone.com/

Twitter
@Fiercelybright1

Other Books by Chelsea Luellon Bolton

Lady of Praise, Lady of Power: Ancient Hymns of the Goddess Aset.

Queen of the Road: Poetry of the Goddess Aset.

Magician, Mother and Queen: A Research Paper on the Goddess Aset.

Divine Words, Divine Praise: Poetry for the Divine Powers.

Lord of Strength and Power: Ancient Hymns for Wepwawet.

Divine Beings, Earthly Praise: Poems for Divine Powers.

Holy Mother, Healer and Queen: Papers on the Feminine Divine.

Sun, Star and Desert Sand: Poems for the Egyptian Gods.

Mother of Magic: Ancient Hymns for Aset.

Queen of the Hearth: An Anthology for Frigga.

She Who Speaks Through Silence: An Anthology for Nephthys.

Flaming Lioness: Ancient Hymns for Egyptian Goddesses.

Forthcoming Titles

Lady of the Temple: Ancient Hymns for Nephthys.

Solar Flares and Sunbeams: An Anthology for Ra.

Mother of Nine: An Anthology for Oya.

Made in United States
North Haven, CT
20 January 2022

15038451R00171